Where Does the Jesus Story Begin?

By the same author

Jesus and the Gospels
Jesus and the Gospels: set of 36 lectures on CD
The Parables of Jesus
Seasons of the Word: Reflections on the Sunday Readings
Impressions of Jesus
The Gospel of Mark
The Gospel of Luke
Emmaus: The Gracious Visit of God according to Luke
Waiting on God
Where Does the Jesus Story Begin? Set of 10 lectures on CD

all available from Redemptorist Publications

Where Does the Jesus Story Begin?

Reflections on the Beginning of the Gospels

Denis McBride

A Redemptorist Publication

Published by **Redemptorist Publications**
A Registered Charity limited by guarantee.
Registered in England 3261721.

Copyright © 2006 Redemptorist Publications

Design: Mono Creative

ISBN-10: 0-85231-329-2
ISBN-13: 978-0-85231-329-9

Front cover image: *La Reproduction Interdite* by René Magritte
© ADAGP, Paris and DACS, London 2006.

Redemptorist Publications has paid DACS' visual creators for the use of their artistic works.

Printed by Cambridge University Press

Alphonsus House Chawton Hampshire GU34 3HQ
Telephone 01420 88222 Fax 01420 88805
rp@rpbooks.co.uk   www.rpbooks.co.uk

For

the Redemptorist community
and the staff at Hawkstone Hall
in gratitude for their support
and good humour

Contents

1 Where do you begin a story?

The promise of story

Every story makes a promise, however implicit, to the readers. Different stories – mysteries, romances, biographies, for example – make different promises to those who would set out on this new journey of the mind: some promise to be entertaining, others informative, while others promise to make their readers feel and think deeply. Through the skill of his or her craft, the writer hopes to engage the readers from the beginning of the story, draw them into a narrative world of conflict where they will meet a variety of characters and situations, lead them to care what happens to the people in the story, show how competing characters and forces collide in a climax, and bring the whole recital to a satisfactory resolution. When the writer achieves this, the promise is delivered and the readers can feel satisfied that their journey has been worth the time and the mental effort.

In the opening paragraph of his Gospel, Luke speaks in the first person as narrator and makes an explicit promise to his friend, Theophilus, and by extension to all his readers:

> Inasmuch as many have undertaken to compile a narrative of the things which have been accomplished among us, just as they were delivered to us by those who from the beginning were eyewitnesses and ministers of the word, it seemed good to me also, having followed all things closely for some time past, to write an orderly account for you, most excellent Theophilus, that you may know the truth concerning the things of which you have been informed (Luke 1:1-4).

In so many words Luke says, "If you read my story you will know the truth about Jesus of Nazareth. My story is not fiction but securely based on those who were eyewitnesses and preachers." This story, the claim goes, while it is not written by an eyewitness, is written with care by a writer who has followed "all things closely". The story is credible because it comes from reliable firsthand witnesses, from those who knew Jesus personally, heard his teaching, witnessed his mighty deeds, and were transformed by his death and resurrection.

The fourth evangelist waits until near the end of his writing to declare his purpose: "that you may believe that Jesus is the Christ, the Son of God, and believing you may have life in his name" (John 20:31). Both Luke (at the beginning of his writing) and John (at the end of his account) promise their readers that they will know the truth about their subject, Jesus Christ.

Mark as narrator announces to us, the readers, that the story he is telling is "The beginning of the Good News about Jesus the Christ, the Son of God" (Mark 1:1). He is the only evangelist to entitle his work, *Euangelion*, Good News, promising his listeners/readers that they will hear or read not only what is "news" but what is essentially good for them. Mark is reporting a story he promises to be a good one, not in the sense that it will be interesting, which it will, but more importantly that it might affect the lives of those who are touched by its power. As Andrew Marr, the BBC journalist, observed:

> All my working life I've been surrounded by "the story" – somewhere out there, day after day, waiting to be discovered. But there is a mystery here. What is a news story? We are perpetually intrigued by the extreme, the gruesome, the outlandish. But there is not a reliable supply of these events . . . So, journalists learn to take the less extraordinary things and fashion them into words that will make them seem like news instead . . . journalists reshape real life, cutting away details, simplifying events, "improving" ordinary speech, sometimes inventing quotes, to create a narrative which will work. It isn't only journalists. Everyone does it, all the time, most unconsciously . . . the impulse to tell stories is hard-wired and fundamental to being human.[1]

Although Mark is not a journalist reporting events as he witnessed them for himself, he has committed himself to tell the story of Jesus of Nazareth in such a way that it can be received and welcomed as good news. Mark will shape what he knows to that end, excluding what he regards as irrelevant to his purpose, sharpening his narrative to catch the interest of the listener/reader, and honour his assurance of delivering good news. That is his declared promise. For the readers of the Gospels, indeed for any readers, to believe the explicit or implicit promise of the writer is an act of trust in the person who makes it; it's to live in expectation, holding fast to the writer's word. And when promises are fulfilled there is a deepening of the original trust. Only the reader can judge if an evangelist's promise has been discharged. Ernest Hemingway could have been commenting on the evangelists' objective when he wrote:

---

[1] A. Marr, *My Trade: A Short History of British Journalism* (London: Pan Books, 2005), 56, 57.

A writer's problem does not change. He himself changes and the world he lives in changes but his problem remains the same. It is always how to write truly and having found what is true, to project it in such a way that it becomes part of the experience of the person who reads it.[2]

Story and belonging

We all live inside the world of story, the narrative of our own lives, one that is personal and one that is public, one that is private to ourselves – no matter how open and direct we are to significant others – and one that is in the public domain. We also live inside a complex web of larger narratives of family, friends, organisations, tribe, nation, race, religion and politics (if any), which add to the accumulation of our personal and social identities. None of us is only one identity: by definition we are a collection of given or assumed identities. Many of these identities were prearranged for us, some are inherited, and a few we make for ourselves. While we can change some of them, many stubbornly remain with us, and throughout our lives we are challenged to accept and do the best with what has been given to us.

If we all have a range of personal and social identities, each of us is formed from a multiplicity of influences that shape the way we think and act and feel. Some of these identities are more significant than others because they have played an influential role in shaping the way we now are. The important identities will differ from person to person, and also from time to time in our lives: we may drop old identities that no longer represent who we are, or we may claim new ones. The important thing is that these identities give us a sense of belonging to a shared story that is larger than our own; they serve to confirm us in who we are, and are perceived to be, in our community and society.

Sometimes our personal identity can be in crisis, when we are unsure or perplexed about who or what we belong to, about our own sense of fitting in to a family or community or country. In an article in *The New Yorker,* Jane Kramer wrote about multiculturalism and Muslim immigrants in Holland, particularly following on the murder of the filmmaker Theo van Gogh. As part of her research Kramer spoke to Paul Scheffer, a well-known Amsterdam intellectual. In the interview he argued that Holland had let its immigrants rot in their own privacy:

---

[2] Quoted in N. Kress, *Beginnings, Middles and Ends* (Cincinnati: F &W Publications, 1993), ii.

We said, "Leave the children their language of origin, leave them their own history, because they're going back." It became a mantra. Twenty years went by and they didn't go back, and it was still a mantra. But once you accept that multicultural argument against teaching them our history, you are excluding them from collective memory, from an enormous chance for renewal. So generation one tried to re-create the fantasy world of home, and generation two had no cultural context, no identification, either with its parents or with the culture here. September 11th gave many of them their narrative. To the extent that radicalization – radical, international Islam – is linked to preventing integration, that may be very difficult to control.[3]

Following the battles between Catholics and Protestants in the seventeenth century in Holland, there ensued an agreement that the two religions would live alongside each other in studied forbearance: you didn't have to love or approve of your neighbours, only tolerate them and allow them to live in peace. Since then the Dutch have become known for their acceptance of difference – what Scheffer calls "wonderful negligence"[4] – but, like other countries in Europe, they are now facing not so much an immigration problem as an identity problem ("no collective memory") following a policy of separation and "toleration" towards immigrants. What do you do when you have second- or third-generation members of such families – born and bred in a country – some of whom feel no loyalty either to that country or to the culture, and certainly not to secular democracy – even sometimes despising its values as morally blurred or utterly abhorrent? What do you do when people elect to live "here" but have no "here" to belong to, choosing their principal identity as belonging to a stateless international religion? With the gradual rise of nationalist parties, including the British Nationalist Party, what do you do when three-quarters of potential BNP supporters believe that "Britain almost seems like a foreign country"?[5] What do you do when some frustrated people call for a halt to new immigration because they believe the government has lost the plot? These questions, among others, are calling out for consideration by numerous governments and religious leaders.

Questions like these are being asked more often, even if they make some people uncomfortable because they sound politically incorrect. It leads some people to ask a further question in the light of living in a multicultural society: "What does it mean to be English?" – substitute your own nationality. Popular books are being written struggling for the

---

[3] J. Kramer, "The Dutch Model: Multiculturalism and Muslim Immigrants" in *The New Yorker* (3 April 2006), 63,64.
[4] Kramer, "The Dutch Model", 64.
[5] George Jones, *The Daily Telegraph* (21 April 2006), 1.

formation of an answer, even if there is disagreement about what it is that makes or confirms someone in a specific nationality, marks him or her as a true national.[6]

What does it mean to be a Jew? What difference is there, say, in being a British Jew, a French Jew, or a German Jew? While Jesus was a Palestinian Jew of the first century — there is hardly disagreement about his race, religion, or nationality — there is a difference in the Gospels about how his Jewishness is portrayed. While the fourth Gospel goes its own way, presenting Jesus and his followers as somehow different from "you Jews", with Jesus himself coming from above (and we will discuss this in part five), there is a general sense that Jesus belonged to his own time, race, religion, culture and land. Given the huge variety of diverse groups and attitudes within first-century Judaism — it was not a monolithic undifferentiated religion — it is hardly surprising that Jesus is presented as an individual, although sometimes non-conformist and critical, who has a clear sense of belonging to the inherited wisdom of the Jews. Like John the Baptist, Jesus belongs to a sacred tradition — one that shapes his teaching and mission.

As we shall see in detail later, the evangelists all attach the person of Jesus to the larger story he lives inside: Mark attaches Jesus' whole ministry through the Isaian prophecy to the great prophetic story of Israel; Matthew devotes the first two chapters to Jesus' identity as a son of Abraham and his belonging to a particular place (kinship and land); in his opening chapters Luke shows Jesus as part of an upright Jewish family who obeys the Law and is recognised by representative figures of Israel; John in his Prologue speaks of the *Logos* (the Word) coming from above to his own people, even if they reject him. Apart from the fourth Gospel, Jesus is not an outsider; he is not an alien from afar or a total renegade; he does not have to invent himself but finds himself as a part of a family, a land, a religion and a culture. He belongs. That belonging is still summarised in the name we remember him by: Jesus of Nazareth.

Story and conflict

While the principal character in all four Gospels is Jesus of Nazareth, he is introduced differently onto the stage each time. Mark introduces us to an adult Jesus who leaves home and travels south to be baptised by John the Baptist; Matthew introduces us to a child whose Jewish roots make him the son of David and the son of Abraham; Luke introduces us to a

---

[6]For example, J. Paxman, *The English: Portrait of a People* (London: Michael Joseph, 1998).

child born of a virgin mother whose roots go back to Adam; John introduces us to the *Logos* that existed with God and was God before the beginning of the world. While the evangelists develop their narrative on different stages, varying from the countryside to the cosmos, they all develop their story of conflict in a similar fashion.

If all stories proceed through conflict – there is no story without one – writers usually establish the conflict early in the story. "Once upon a time everyone lived happily every after" is not a story for the simple reason that there is no conflict. Conflict is friction, tension, opposition: it is the driving force of story. If there is nothing in a story to fight against, nothing to win, nothing to lose, why would anyone bother reading on? If the principal character never struggles, is never tested by adversity, never battles against outside forces, the story goes nowhere.

Conflict is not just essential to the development of a story – it is the essence of every story. What makes a story interesting and engaging is the conflict that stands between the protagonist and his or her goal. Readers want to become involved in the hero's personal battle to achieve a specific goal, and if the writer successfully engages the readers in that struggle they will worry about whether or not the hero can actually reach this goal. Conflict stimulates that worry. Another way of looking at conflict is to think of it as a barrier: conflict is what stands in the way of the protagonist; it is the force that needs to be overcome if the story is to reach a successful conclusion. Conflict is when two forces are in opposition to each other. These forces can be personal, internal, social, physical or elemental.

There are different kinds of conflict developed in narrative writing, reflecting the diverse conflicts we all face in the course of daily living:

- **Personal or inter-personal conflict** emerges when there is tension between the protagonist and other characters in the story: this is evident in the Gospels not only between Jesus and his opponents but between Jesus and his own family and disciples.

- **Internal conflict** is not with other characters in the story, though it can affect them, but within the protagonist when he or she suffers some inner turmoil: this can be seen in the Synoptic accounts of Gethsemane, where Jesus is suffering acute anxiety and isolation before his arrest. Internal conflict adds complexity to the external conflict, and the external conflict forces internal choices and changes.

Social conflict is present in stories between the hero and the values or customs of the surrounding society or between the hero and authority figures: this is clear throughout the sweep of the Gospel narratives, culminating in Jesus' conviction by the religious and civil authorities and his public execution.

Physical conflict is present in stories when the leading character struggles with his or her bodily strength while facing a time of trial: this feat of physical endurance is apparent throughout the passion narratives.

Finally, there is sometimes **elemental conflict** in stories between the protagonist and the environment or between the protagonist and the forces of evil: in the Gospels this conflict is clearly displayed in the temptations in the wilderness, the nature miracles, and the escalating battle with Satan and the demonic forces.

We begin to understand the protagonist through seeing how he or she responds to conflict. How individuals react to challenging situations defines their character. We respond to how characters deal with conflict because we have to relate to conflict in our own lives: it is part of our everyday living to cope with conflict and endure struggle. How Jesus in the Gospel narratives faces a variety of conflicts helps us not only to understand his character and values but gain perspective on our own lives; the same is true as we watch the disciples facing their own tensions. If we disagree with the choices a character makes when dealing with conflict, like Judas for example, we can form negative opinions about that individual. If we admire the choices characters make, like the women followers who stubbornly stay with Jesus through crucifixion and death, we admire them more. The way people face conflict evokes our admiration or disapproval; it helps us choose which character to support in the drama of action.

Throughout their narratives the evangelists present us with a variety of characters and a variety of conflicts. None of them keeps his attention exclusively focused on Jesus because the Gospel story each of them is writing is one that *shows* who Jesus is through the drama of interaction with others. The evangelists have to follow the old adage: "Don't tell me, show me!" How other people react to what Jesus does and says is an essential part of the drama. Thus there is no paragraph in the Gospels where Jesus is alone: even in the wilderness, where he goes to be alone, the inner conflict he faces is developed through a story of interaction with Satan. Who he is, his identity, is revealed through what he does and says, and also how he relates to people and events. While John *tells* us who Jesus is in the grand statement of his Prologue, he develops that statement through story in the rest of his narrative. While dogmatic theologians can declare truth in statements, evangelists have to show truth through story: their chosen medium is story not essay, narrative not treatise.

Story focuses on the world of the particular, gathering details of time, place, people and events, to give colour and shape and substance to the telling. By contrast, statements convey general truths about people, events and the world; they focus on meaning. For example:

> **Statement:** On average, four people are killed every year on Ben Nevis, the highest mountain in Britain.

> **Story:** Last December, Ludwig Ratzinger, an amateur climber from Bonn in Germany, was killed on the Orion Face of Ben Nevis, after he was lost in the fog and suffered a fatal fall.

Stories draw us into particular events that happen to specific people at a definite time: particularity is at the heart of every story. By using story the evangelists hope to draw us into the particular first-century Palestinian world of their narrative rather than keep us as spectators of a distant drama. Where would we locate ourselves inside this story? Who would we stand beside? How would we react to what Jesus is doing or saying? Listening to the different assessments of Jesus offered throughout the narrative by different people, who would we say he is? Who do we agree with in the various confrontations? When Jesus is led away and handed over to the authorities, how would we react? Who would we follow? When would we leave?

The evangelists hope that the story they write will engage us and provoke a measure of internal conflict within us: if this story is true, what difference does it make in my life? If we believe after reading Luke's Gospel that the evangelist has delivered on his explicit promise – "that you may know the truth concerning the things of which you have been informed" – Luke's kept promise becomes our enduring challenge. Where Luke's story finishes, ours could begin anew.

Choosing a beginning

Where do you begin? This is a question that has intrigued me as both a lecturer and a writer: how do you make a start? How do you get going? Anyone who has written a speech or a lecture or a book – even a letter –

has to make the decision about where to begin. How do you start the story in such a way that will engage people's attention and command their interest from the beginning? If you are writing someone else's story, what point do you choose to make the beginning of that story? What incident in the life of your subject do you select as an appropriate introduction to draw the reader into your narrative?

What is your name? Where were you born? What is the date of your birth? Who are your mother and father? Who are your brothers and sisters? Do you have a heart condition in your family? What is your family's medical history? These are simple questions that we are asked throughout life, but what if we cannot provide the answers because we do not know? In her book, *Nobody's Child,* the journalist Kate Adie explores the fate of foundlings – those children abandoned by their parents, without any knowledge of who they might be, or even a name to call their own – and she writes with great sensitivity about a subject that is close to her heart, since she was adopted herself. Most foundlings do not know where they were born, only the place where they were found, as with Christine Simms:

> I was found in a paper bag in the back of a London cab. It was parked in William IV Street near the Strand. There's a big white building there which is now a police station, but it was then the Charing Cross Hospital. This was 8 December 1949, and I was wrapped in a green woollen cardigan. I was described as "a few hours old"...
>
> The newspaper account said that the taxi driver had left his cab to have a cup of tea, and he'd left the window open. He got back in the cab and he heard me – this baby – and he turned round and lo and behold, there I was. I was taken to Charing Cross Hospital. There was an article in the *News of the World* and the *Evening Standard,* but nobody came forward.[7]

Christine only learned this story years later, at the funeral of her adoptive mother in 1993. She checked the newspaper cuttings and for the first time saw a photograph of herself, the foundling, in the arms of a nurse. Although she tracked down the nurse through the Retired Nurses' Foundation, and tried to do the same, without success, with the taxi driver, after a long time searching through records, even publicising her story through radio and television, she had no success in discovering her past – something which she has accepted. As she noted in the interview: "I've had to make my own way – and I quite like that, so I think there

---

[7] K. Adie, *Nobody's Child: Who Are You When You Don't Know Your Past?* (London: Hodder & Stoughton, 2005), 41.

are positive aspects . . . I *would* love to know who my mother was, and I know I shan't."[8]

The majority of biographies and autobiographies elect to begin at the obvious place, in a birth story, introducing the readers to the parents of their subject, the time of birth, the place, and any telling circumstances surrounding the beginning of the life story. When people have made a name for themselves in public life, there is a tendency to seek the germ of that career somewhere in childhood; it is almost impossible, however, apart from figures of royalty whose fame relies on their birth into a particular family, to find it in the birth itself. Since birth stories – everyone has one – rarely capture the flavour of a future life, some writers make a different beginning, choosing instead an incident in the life of their subject that captures a characteristic quality the reader will meet throughout the narrative. For example, in Stephen McGinty's *This Turbulent Priest: The Life of Cardinal Winning,* the author opens on page one of his biography with the following story:

> If ever an incident encapsulated the character of Cardinal Thomas Joseph Winning, it was a meeting with Derry Irvine, the Lord Chancellor. The Archbishop of Glasgow had travelled to London in 1999 to meet Britain's most powerful lawmaker, in order to raise concerns over the issue of bioethics. After a long wait in the outer chambers of the Lord Chancellor's office at the House of Lords, the Cardinal spotted Irvine striding towards him, woollen wig flowing, ruffled shirt tucked in place, breeches and silk stockings meeting neatly at the knee, and patent leather shoes buffed to a brilliant shine, offset by silver buckles. As Irvine breezed past, offering the Cardinal the briefest of nods, Winning nudged Ronnie Convery, his current-affairs adviser, and said: "If that's the Lord Chancellor, can you imagine what God looks like?"[9]

McGinty chose this incident to open his narrative because it offers the reader an immediate insight into the Cardinal who, even though he was an authority figure himself as a prince of the Church, was a miner's son and a humorist inclined to cartoon pompous authority, an outsider who was a constant critic of government. The story makes a good beginning because it captures in summary the kind of person the Archbishop revealed himself to be in public life, the "turbulent priest" of the book's title, an epithet originally ascribed to another archbishop – Thomas à Becket who had, paradoxically, also been Lord Chancellor – by King Henry II.

---

[8] Adie, *Nobody's Child,* 45.

[9] S. McGinty, *This Turbulent Priest: The Life of Cardinal Winning* (London: HarperCollins, 2003), 1.

Life stories have many beginnings, the more obvious being birth, schooling, leaving home, beginning relationships, starting a job, settling into a partnership or single life or marriage, beginning a family, moving to new places, and retirement. There can, of course, be other new beginnings in disruptive experiences: death of a loved one, divorce, unemployment, exposure of some flaw in the media, being dismissed from your job, etc. Some new beginnings are not of our choosing and are forced upon us by circumstances, but they can have the weight of shaping a future life. Sometimes life is interrupted by unforeseen events, and the interruption prompts a new beginning and a new story.

In the biblical narrative you often meet people *in medias res* – their story begins in the middle of things – when their life is interrupted by the unexpected. In Matthew's portrait of Joseph, for instance, the evangelist's chosen Jewish protagonist for the opening of his narrative is portrayed as having already entered into the formal contract of betrothal to Mary; the second part of the contract, living together, has yet to take place. Although the couple are not living together, Matthew refers to Joseph as Mary's husband (Matthew 1:19). The new husband discovers the shocking news that his wife is pregnant outside their relationship: in a world of uncertainties he knows one thing for sure, that he is not the father. While we are told by the evangelist how this came to be in verse 18, Joseph remains in the dark. We the readers are wiser than the protagonist in the story.

We first meet Joseph, a righteous man, in personal anguish at this aching discovery. What to do? He resolves not to take Mary to court to face a public inquiry before the rigour of the Law, but to divorce her quietly, thus avoiding a public spectacle and the inevitable resultant shame. Before he implements his plan, however, his life is interrupted again by an annunciation in a dream, explaining what we already know and what he needs to know – that the child "conceived in her is of the Holy Spirit" (Matthew 1:20).

Will Joseph follow his natural instincts or pursue the stuff of dreams? Will he separate himself from Mary and carve out a new life for himself or take her to his home in Bethlehem as his wife? Will *he* give the name to this child, as commanded in the dream, thus becoming the child's legal father? Or will the delicate revelation in the dark of night fade in the gathering glow of the morning light?

When Joseph wakes he decides to follow the dream, not his instincts, a decision that will change his life for ever. Matthew's brief narrative of this upright Jewish man, who comes to welcome the unexpected and comes to adjust his life to God's revelation, stands in dramatic contrast to the Jewish religious authorities in Jerusalem who, when they are unexpectedly confronted with magi seeking the address of the King of the Jews and themselves uncover the address as revealed in scripture (Matthew 2:5-6), do not follow the revelation but leave it unheeded on the scroll on which they found it. Joseph is Matthew's outstanding Jewish hero in his infancy narrative. For the writer, Joseph's real story begins as a life interrupted by the unexpected: while most wives have to adjust to their husbands' plans, Joseph is startled by a contrary demand, which he learns to accept as a new beginning.

A modern example of a story that begins with life interrupted is Carlos Eire's evocative memoir, *Waiting for Snow in Havana*. On 1 January 1959, in Cuba, the cigar-smoking guerrilla Fidel Castro ousted President Batista: suddenly Christmas was made illegal and political dissent led to imprisonment. Life changed radically for every Cuban. Carlos Eire begins his story:

> The world changed while I slept, and much to my surprise, no one had consulted me. That's how it would always be from that day forward. Of course, that's the way it had been all along. I just didn't know it until that morning. Surprise upon surprise: some good, some evil, most somewhere in between. And always without my consent. I was barely eight years old.[10]

Eire begins his story with life interrupted: his boyhood was ravaged by the Cuban revolution and his life would be for ever changed by the experience of loss and separation. In 1962 he was one of 14,000 unaccompanied children airlifted out of Cuba, exiled from his family and country. He lived in a series of foster homes until he was reunited with his mother in Chicago after three years. He has never returned to Cuba, but he explained: "the world that exists in my memory is so vivid perhaps because I have given up on the idea of ever reclaiming it . . . that world survives in my mind and in my soul, intact".[11]

Carlos Eire is currently a professor of history and religion at Yale University, a modern American man. Given who he is today, where did *that* story start? He chooses not to begin the story with his birth: who he is today was not decided by his birth into a particular family, but, he

---

[10] C. Eire, *Waiting for Snow in Havana: Confessions of a Cuban Boy* (New York: Free Press, 2003), 1.
[11] Eire, *Waiting for Snow*, 390.

claims, by what happened on the night of 1 January 1959, the beginning of the Cuban revolution: "the world changed while I slept". For him the Castro regime changed everything; the revolution turned his homeland into paradise lost and catapulted him in a new direction to faraway places, placing him on a road that he would not otherwise have taken. That new road was to lead him to who he is today.

Alone among the evangelists, Mark says that the Jesus story really begins when he leaves home as an adult and travels south to meet John the Baptist. While we will look at Mark's story of the baptism later, the new road that Jesus takes will lead him to a life that is dramatically different from the one he has been leading heretofore. Jesus is attracted by the preaching and baptising ministry of this independent prophet who is already attracting crowds of people from Judea and Jerusalem. The measure of John's influence on Jesus is seen by Jesus' change: when he leaves John he begins to lead the life of an independent prophet and teacher, a change that is noticed but not welcomed with approval when he returns to his home town of Nazareth: "'Where did this man get all this? What is the wisdom given to him? What mighty works are wrought by his hands! Is not this the carpenter, the son of Mary and brother of James and Joses and Judas and Simon, and are not his sisters here with us?' And they took offence at him" (Mark 6:2-3).

New beginnings in life are not always greeted with approval or welcomed with applause. Jesus leaves his hometown and in the Gospel narrative never returns again, but he does maintain the lifestyle of a wandering prophet and teacher until the end of his life. That resolute change of life indicates that Jesus made a critical choice and persisted in that choice for the rest of his life: that choice, Mark argues, goes back to the time of John the Baptist. For Mark, that is the real beginning of the Jesus story.

Telling someone else's story

Recently I was reading a book called *Sons and Mothers,* a series of brief portraits where mothers write about their sons and sons write about their mothers. One son described his mother as an unsmiling piece of granite, who was as hard as she was immovable. Michael Bywater, a journalist for the *Independent on Sunday,* wrote in a more reflective tone:

> It is difficult to glimpse the truth of another's life, even your mother's, and it is hard to set it down on paper. We demand to read

about characters; or we demand plot, conflict, and drama. The telling of an ordinary life, lived under simple domestic lighting, is too homely a story for our modern ears. Like Scottish food or sensible shoes, it fails to excite . . . But it's the uncomplicated things that matter in life: a secure home, a family well-cared for, food on the table, warmth, and above all the ancient virtues of love, honesty, and reliability.[12]

Biographers and journalists rarely write about ordinary people – who among the original followers of Jesus, for example, would have merited a modern biography, apart from Peter and Judas? There is a presumption against ordinariness when it comes to choosing a subject to write about, the presumption being that ordinariness is synonymous with dullness, and that "the telling of an ordinary life" would evoke little or no interest in readers. Since few lives are lived out on a spectacular plane or progress according to some master narrative plan, it can be difficult to find a governing template that will hold a life story together. Some biographers are compelled to fabricate an overarching meaning to a life story by imposing some reassuring pattern of cause and effect that will satisfy the reader's hunger for pattern. But we know from our own experience that people's lives can be a collection of random incidents with events succeeding one another in what appears to be a world of accident and contingency. Hence the modern cry, "Get a life!"

In a critique of biographical narrative, Dean S. Fish writes:

Although biographies are a staple in bookstores and a favorite of reviewers, I confess that I rarely pick one up and almost never finish it when I do. Beginning a biography always makes me queasy, and queasiness turns into something close to a feeling of illness by the time I reach the third sentence.

The first sentence is usually O.K. It goes something like this: "On the fifth of May, 1879, in a small town in Ohio, John Smith was born to Aaron and Sarah Smith in the main house of their family farm." Nothing much to quarrel with there, but nothing much to hold a reader's interest either. Interest is supposed to be supplied by the second sentence, which might be, "It was a year of drought, and the collapse of farm prices seemed imminent." Or, "Memories of the Civil War were still strong, and quarrels between partisans often erupted in the inns and ale-houses of southern Ohio."

---

[12] M. & V. Glendinning (eds), *Sons and Mothers* (London: Virago, 1996), 198, 206.

It is with this second sentence, no matter what it is, that a gap opens up and a question is implied. What connects the first and second sentences? What is the relationship between the birth of John Smith and the imminent collapse of farm prices or post-Civil War tensions or anything else?

Presumably the gap will be filled or at least begin to be filled by the third sentence, but in fact the third sentence only widens the gap. When it arrives you realize that it could have been almost anything. "Little did little John know... " Or, "Only years later would it become clear... " Or, "Meanwhile, in another part of the country ..." And if the third sentence could be almost anything, so could the fourth and the fifth, and on and on, with nothing stopping the spiral sprawl of unconvincing speculation except the occasional sentence that, in its solidity and flatness, reminds you of the first: "John Smith married Betsy Jones in the fall of 1901." Or, "On Dec. 10, 1944, he was hit by lightning and died immediately."

It's the stuff in between that's the problem. You know what it's supposed to do – it's supposed to supply the explanatory structure that links and gives depth to the bare recital of dated events – but all it really does is call attention to the stretch and strain of conceptual bridges that are not connecting.[13]

Fish's philosophical presupposition is that we live in a world of contingency, something he sees denied in almost every biography he has tried to read where contingency is replaced with explanatory structure, ending up with an orderly narrative of cause and effect, where the biographer supplies transitions and analyses that are fundamentally constructions of his imagination. Fish's voice is a particularly modern one: everything is provisional and makeshift; the progress of a life with its myriad and complicated choices defies real explanation. Biographers, by compulsion, he seems to argue, feel constrained to construct a performance out of a life that is by definition accidental.

While few scholars would argue that the Gospels could be considered as biographies in the modern sense, there has been an interesting development over recent years in understanding the Gospel genre. The genre "Gospel" was regarded for nearly a century as a unique literary type that Christianity had contributed to ancient literature. In recent times, however, this consensus has broken down: in particular, the close relationship of the genre "Gospel" to the genre of ancient biography has

---

[13] S. Fish, "Just Published: Minutiae Without Meaning", *New York Times,* 7 September 1999, op. ed. page.

been convincingly demonstrated.[14]   A new consensus is emerging that regards the Christian genre of "Gospel" as a mixed genre composed of Old Testament hagiography and Hellenistic biography.

Professor Lawrence Wills is particularly helpful. He argues that the genre that best describes the Gospels is biography, but a biography that follows an Israelite pattern as much as it does a Greco-Roman pattern. Whereas Greco-Roman biography emphasises the life, virtues and accomplishments of the central character, Israelite biography emphasises God's call of the central character, his governing mission and the accomplishment of his objective. Wills concludes that "the comparison of the Gospels with biographies does not require an adjustment of what we mean by 'Gospel' (as was once believed), but may entail an adjustment of what we mean by 'biography'."[15]   While few would dispute that the Gospel genre is derived to some extent from the kerygma (early preaching) and is shaped by the message it seeks to communicate as Good News, yet the genre has certain links to other literature, both Jewish and Greco-Roman.

In concert with Israelite biography, the four canonical Gospels place emphasis on Jesus accomplishing God's mission, a paradigm that dominates the movement of his life and public ministry. For the evangelists, that belief provides their writing with an overarching meaning, a master narrative, one that is by definition neither makeshift nor accidental. It is indeed that master narrative that makes sense of what might otherwise appear in the Gospel narrative as random choices, foolhardy risks and imprudent alliances. What is missing in Fish's modern world of biography is omnipresent in the ancient Gospel world of the Jesus story, a governing purpose that unites character and plot, event and meaning, cause and effect, life and death.

Telling your own story

Why do we do the things we do? How have we ended up where we are today? Trying to answer that question for myself is proving an uneasy quest: as a Redemptorist looking back at my own story, trying to uncover why I chose the Redemptorist road as a way to life, I find it an exercise in creative memory. Reviewing our own past, we like to believe that our choices were free of desperation or compulsion; we want to believe that who we are is the fruit of high-minded decisions inspired by God and his angels. Our need for narrative sense makes us impose a pattern on the fitfulness of the past so that it all reads like a sensible story. We can all rewrite our infancy narrative to build a ground of explanation for who

---

[14] See, for example, an excellent scholarly discussion that argues analogies between the Gospel genre and Jewish and Greco-Roman literature: L. Wills, *The Quest of the Historical Gospel: Mark, John and the Origins of the Gospel Genre* (London: Routledge, 1997); see also R. A. Burridge, *What are the Gospels? A Comparison with Graeco-Roman Biography* (Grand Rapids: Eerdmans, 2004).
[15] Wills, *Quest*, 17.

we have turned out to be. Like St Paul who wrote to the Galatians: "God, who had set me apart before I was born and called me through his grace…" (Galatians 1:15). If God chose Paul while he was in his mother's womb, it took some time for the accomplished persecutor to catch up with his apostolic beginning.

Once upon a time I met a man in a Redemptorist habit who impressed me. He came to give a retreat at the college, a junior seminary in Scotland, where I was training for the secular priesthood. I was sixteen at the time. We greeted his arrival with the tired cynicism of youth, expecting to be bored by more religion. He was a surprise. His enormous natural gifts were put at the service of preaching the Gospel and he succeeded in helping us believe that the Gospel could make a difference to the way we breathed and behaved. He didn't seem like the other priests: where they appeared tame and institutionalised, he appeared wild and free; when they were stuck teaching geography and mathematics in a seminary, he was wandering the country preaching Good News. I was not only impressed by him, I wanted to be like him.

Nothing happened for a while. At the end of the school year, my form-master told me that I was being asked to leave: my academic work had not been up to standard; I was a lazy student, interested only in sports; I had been caught too often wasting my study periods reading fiction instead of doing assignments. All this, I must admit, was perfectly true, but the rejection was hard to accept. I still believed, against the evidence, that I had the makings of a priest; the desire was still alive and well. My form-master knew I was impressed by the visiting Redemptorist. The archdiocese of Glasgow did not want me; perhaps the Redemptorists might have room for the likes of me.

Rejection was my driving force for becoming a Redemptorist. I'm not sure what a psychiatrist or an angel would think about that as a nurturing ground for a religious vocation, but rejection, together with my desire to be a priest, impelled me into the Congregation. When I applied, I was interviewed and accepted – provided I first spent a year at a college in Wales because I was too young to enter the novitiate. That year in Wales I enjoyed enormously; the studies were easy and the freedom was cosmic compared to the junior seminary. I felt happy because I was on the road that would lead me to becoming like that Redemptorist I had met once upon a time.

Where would you choose to begin your own story? Given who you are today, where did *that* story begin?

The distinguished novelist John Irving, in an interview for *Writer's Workshop* at the University of South Carolina, reported on the internet, shared with the students his unusual technique of writing last things first. "I have to write last sentences", he explained, "in order to get a viewpoint or voice for the rest of the work. How do you know how to begin a story if you don't know who's dead at the end of it?" Knowing the ending shapes the way the beginning is crafted. By definition, however, we do not know how our own life stories will end so we choose a beginning without knowing what the final act will be.

Recently when I was lecturing in South Africa I visited the Apartheid Museum in Johannesburg, which had a special exhibition on storytelling your life. The exhibition was done by Khulumani support groups of Western Cape in South Africa: *khulumani* is a Zulu word, meaning to tell the story to a group of people. The support groups use body maps and memory cloths to tell stories of their suffering under apartheid. The body maps are life-size images of human bodies used to explore and also to reflect on how people see themselves. At the beginning of the process people work in pairs: you lie down on a piece of large paper and the other person traces the outline of your body. The process moves from the physical to the spiritual:

1. The physical body is outlined: your unique individual shape. Only you. This story will move from the physical shape you are to the psychological/spiritual shape you are in. But it is the outline of the body that is the entry point, working with what people know best – the outside of themselves. This is the basic you, the outline.

2. In a step-by-step process, the individuals explore the layers of their bodies starting with the surface – colour, face, scars, wounds, birthmarks, etc. – what others can see. This is the visible self, the public self.

3. They then move deeper beneath the skin to organs and systems of the body, such as bones, heart, blood, etc. What is your energy here, and what has been wounded or lost?

4. This leads on to an exploration of their ideas about their own identity: their beauty, their health, their family, the places they have lived, the key

experiences they have had, and their symbols of hope. The people draw this or little explanatory notes on the side of the figure are written.

5. On the final day of the workshop, the participants place their body map on the floor in the middle of the group, and they stand up and tell the story: *khulumani*. They share their identity and life story with the other members of the group. In all this, there is the belief that there will be release and liberation through the telling of the story.

In the exhibition they had examples of the final drawings people made, their body maps and memory cloths, and also tapes were playing of the people's stories that interpreted the drawings. The voices supported the drawings. I found it a deeply moving experience and a simple way of helping people to tell their story. The scars that people marked on their drawings were often on the inside, not on the outside of the body. Looking at the body maps I thought that they were an echo of an older story – the body map of Jesus – the enduring figure of the crucified one, the image that is most associated with Jesus, one that recalls Jesus not as a powerful teacher or healer but as a vulnerable human being.

The frame of the writing

The South African journalist Rian Malan shared his personal story of struggle in his country's apartheid years. In 1977 he fled his homeland to live in the United States. Eight years later he returned from voluntary exile to face his family history, his conscience, himself, and to write *My Traitor's Heart*. He belonged to a traditional and hated Afrikaner family, the Malans, and found himself totally at odds with the history he had inherited: he was the family's renegade, the one who had betrayed the values of his ancestors by becoming a *kafferboetie* ("brother of blacks", "nigger-lover").

He sets the stage for the readers by introducing them to key ancestors:

> I am a Malan, descendant of Jacques Malan, a Huguenot who fled the France of Louis XIV to escape being put to the sword for his Protestant faith. He sought refuge among the Dutch, only to be put aboard ship in 1688 and sent to the Dark Continent, to the rude Dutch colony of the Cape of Good Hope. Jacques the Huguenot was the first Malan in Africa. In the centuries since, a Malan has been present at all the great drama and turning points in the history of the Afrikaner tribe.[16]

---

[16] R. Malan, *My Traitor's Heart* (London: Vintage, 1991), 13.

He goes on to note a litany of Malans who played their part in the first Afrikaner rebellion against the British, the Voortrekkers' mission into the heart of Africa, the battle of Blood River, and the Second War of Freedom, which ended in defeat by the British. He brings the story into modern times with Daniel François Malan:

> His Afrikaner Nationalist Party came to power in 1948, vowing to throw off the imperial British yoke and devise a final solution for the "native question". This final solution was apartheid, a gridlock of more than a hundred laws designed to keep blacks and whites forever separate and to ensure that blacks remained in their God-ordained place, hewers of wood and drawers of water, for ever and ever.
>
> This fate was unacceptable to blacks, so they rose against us in earnest in 1976 . . . In this era, too, the destiny of the tribe is in the hands of a Malan – General Magnus Malan, minister of defence.[17]

All of us are born into a family, a tribe or region, a culture, a language group, a country, a time: none of this is of our own choosing, since it is all given to us, and what is given makes its cumulative mark on who we are. So much of who we are is what is given to us; we inherit a whole range of personal and social identities and it can take us what seems an age to determine the kind of person we want to be. Rian Malan chooses the frame of his story well, going back to another time (the seventeenth century) and another place (France) to set the stage of conflict for his personal story. That frame clearly colours the reading of the whole story.

How far back in history would you go to help the reader understand your own story? How far back *could* you go? How important are your ancestors in the formation of your self-identity? Or is there another frame or scaffold – political, religious, or social – which would better explain to the reader the purpose of your life? We will look in some detail later at the dramatically different frames into which the evangelists insert their story of Jesus and how their individual choice of frame influences the shape of their story; we will just note those frames here.

Each evangelist has to decide not only where to begin the story of Jesus, but to supply an outer frame of the Jesus story. The four evangelists answer that question in their own distinct ways. They all knew Jesus was a Jew, that his first disciples were Jews, and that Christianity claimed to be the fulfilment of the Jewish scriptures. The past of the movement was Jewish, so the new story of Jesus had somehow to be connected to that past or to a time beyond it.

---

[17] Malan, *My Traitor's Heart*, 15.

Mark   *back to Isaiah*   the prophetic story

Mark opens his Gospel by building a bridge back to the Jewish scriptures through the prophecy of Isaiah, eighth century BC. That prophecy is secured in the present tense in the person and ministry of John the Baptist. Jesus first appears on Mark's stage as an adult who leaves home in Nazareth and journeys south to join the multitudes being baptised by the wilderness prophet. The breathless pace of Mark's Gospel begins in the midst of ongoing drama – as ancient prophecy is fulfilled, as John heralds an unknown follower, and as Jesus appears from obscurity to begin his prophetic mission.

Matthew   *back to Abraham*   the Jewish story

Matthew begins his Gospel by announcing the identity of Jesus as "son of David, son of Abraham". He proceeds at a leisurely pace with Abraham, nineteenth-century BC, and anchors the identity of Jesus in the Jewish tradition as he catalogues the names of Jesus' weird and wonderful ancestors. God's curious choices include cheats, prostitutes, thieves, adulterers and murderers – illustrating through biography that God's salvation comes through the foolish and the fragile, the crooked and the cracked. Anyone can play a part in God's plan, which finds its fulfilment in Jesus, who is called Christ.

Luke   *back to Adam*   the human story

Luke builds his bridge back to the Jewish scriptures by introducing us to four ancient characters: Zechariah, Elizabeth, Simeon and Anna. While their story is focused in sacred space, in the Temple, the story of Jesus transpires in secular space; first in the village of Nazareth and then in the town of Bethlehem. Later, in his genealogy, Luke presses the ancestry of Jesus back beyond the reaches of the Jewish story to the beginning of the human story in Adam, son of God. This original human connection is grounded in the belief that Jesus is not only the glory of Israel but a light for all nations.

John   *back to the beginning*   the divine story

John's Gospel begins not with an adult Jesus by the river Jordan or a newborn baby in Bethlehem, but before the beginning of the world. For John, the details of Jesus' earthly beginnings are irrelevant – no mother is introduced, no time is recorded, no place is noted, no witnesses are named – because his true origin is beyond the cosmos: "In the beginning was the Word, and the Word was with God, and the Word was God." John goes back beyond the *prophetic story* and *the Jewish story* and *the human story*, to rework Genesis and anchor the beginning of the Jesus story in the originality of God.

The evangelists not only choose different beginning points for the personal story of Jesus, they also choose different outer frames for that narrative, which will shape the way they write their accounts. If you were the first missionary to a tribe who had never heard anything about Jesus, where would you begin the story? Where would you say the Jesus story really started? And what outer frame would you place your story in? How would you fit the Jesus story into the wider story of God's salvation?

2 The beginning of Mark

Introduction

Mark wrote his Gospel around AD 70, which was the year the Temple in Jerusalem was destroyed by the Romans. Before Mark's Gospel a variety of traditions had circulated independently about Jesus, probably in written as well as in oral form. Mark appears to be the first Christian writer to shape traditions of Jesus' deeds and words and the major events of his public life into a narrative that led inexorably to the cross. He is the only evangelist to call his narrative "Gospel". The evangelist devotes a third of his narrative to the final week of Jesus' life; thus everything that is said about Jesus is interpreted under the rubric of his passion and death. In Mark's account no one inside the story understands Jesus until his death: the first human voice to recognise the identity of Jesus is the centurion at the foot of the cross. Jesus' identity is revealed only when his destiny is fulfilled on the cross.

This deliberate emphasis on the suffering of Jesus and his followers (8:34-37) might indicate that Mark is writing for a community facing the threat of persecution: this threat, as Mark will stubbornly and fervently point out, does not render their faith in Jesus useless; rather this real threat calls for an endurance that will surely lead to salvation (13:9-13). Despite the total lack of direct evidence in the Gospel, the scholarly presumption is that Mark was addressing a specific community. A number of places have been proposed for the location of the writing of the Gospel, including Rome, Alexandria and southern Syria.

There is no internal evidence, however, to help the reader identify either a specific community or a specific location, though the Greek of Mark, peppered with Latinisms (of a military, legal and economic nature associated with Roman power) and idiomatic usages, is that of a second-language user. Mary Ann Tolbert, in the company of a number of scholars, identifies Rome as the locale of Mark, speculates that as the Flavian persecutions made public preaching of Christianity impossible, a text capable of being read in a household setting by someone of moderate literacy, such as the Gospel of Mark, was a practical alternative to the danger of public preaching.[1]

If Mark *was* addressing Roman Christians, he was writing for a community that had already suffered persecution and probably lived in

---

[1] M. Tolbert, *Sowing the Gospel: Mark's World in Literary-Historical Perspective* (Minneapolis: Fortress Press, 1989), 305.

fear of more of the same. For the last three years of Nero's reign (AD 65–68), being a Christian was a capital crime in Rome. During that time the Christian community had to face the reality of misrepresentation, betrayal, arrest, false accusation, persecution and violent death – including the execution of Peter and Paul. Clearly the Roman Church needed strengthening after its own time of suffering and passion. Although it seems unlikely that persecution was the precipitating cause for Mark's writing, his Gospel would have addressed such a community in its time of uncertainty. There is a warning that some who receive the word will "endure for a while; then, when tribulation or persecution arises on account of the word, immediately they fall away" (4:17). In 13:9-13 the followers of Jesus are warned explicitly about persecution:

they will deliver you up to councils

you will be beaten in synagogues

you will stand before governors and kings for my sake

they will bring you to trial and deliver you up

family members will betray one another

you will be hated for my name's sake

he who endures to the end will be saved.

That catalogue of suffering is originally told in the passion story of Jesus. For Mark, the pattern of Jesus' passion merges into the experience of his followers, just as his followers can see something of their own experience reflected in the suffering of Jesus. The threat of suffering is introduced early in 3:6 with the Pharisees and the Herodians plotting together about the best way to destroy Jesus: this threat looms over the whole narrative. The three formal prophecies of the passion punctuate the approach to the climax of the Gospel, and each is followed by a pronouncement that the disciples must follow a similar path.

Following the first passion prophecy, Peter tries to divert Jesus and is strongly rebuked: "Get behind me, Satan!" (8:33). The disciples must renounce themselves and take up *their* cross. Following the second prophecy the disciples ignore its content and begin their own seminar on precedence in the kingdom (9:32-34). After the third prophecy the sons of Zebedee approach Jesus to secure the chief places in the kingdom, provoking Jesus' reply that he can offer them only a cup of suffering (10:35-39). Each time Jesus speaks of his own suffering, Mark demonstrates the reluctance of the disciples to accept the message, leading to Jesus' insistence that they must share his suffering.

The distinctive turning-point of Mark's Gospel is the scene at Caesarea Philippi (8:27-30). For the first part of the Gospel the disciples are slowly coming to a recognition of Jesus as Messiah; after Caesarea Philippi they are slowly coming to grasp that Jesus' messiahship involves suffering. The disciples seem to be chronically dull, and their failure seems to get progressively worse, culminating in their abrupt abandonment of Jesus and in Peter's denial. Unlike later Gospels, Mark has no resurrection story of reconciliation between Jesus and the disciples and no missionary commission.

If the passion of Jesus becomes the interpretative key that opens up the mystery of his identity, so the passion of those who come after him will indicate their true identity as his followers. In hearing the Gospel, Mark's community is helped to see that their own suffering, like the story of Jesus' suffering, is not some catastrophic mischance that is devoid of meaning, but a chronicle of salvation that rested within the prophecies of Jesus and God's providence.

The beginning: Jesus' identity is announced

In the prologues of the four Gospels each evangelist takes his hearers/readers into his confidence and discloses to them the identity of Jesus; this always happens before we meet Jesus as the protagonist of the story. None of the evangelists retains this revelation for later use, either in a revelatory climax or at the conclusion of the story: wherever the Gospel begins, the evangelists announce who Jesus is. While the information is given to us the readers, it is not available to the participants in the story. We the readers, with the evangelists as our guides, are always wiser than the participants in the story because we are interpreting the unfolding drama through the privileged viewpoint of the writers.

Although the writer of the first Gospel is anonymous, he is not invisible: he steps onto the stage, like the Chorus in Shakespeare's *Henry V*, to set the scene and introduce the drama about to unfold. Mark as narrator announces to us, the readers, that the story he is telling is "the beginning of the Gospel of Jesus Christ, the Son of God" (1:1). *Euangelion* proclamations, announcements of good news, of the early Roman period were common propaganda tools in the cult of the emperor. The Priene inscription (9 BC) in Asia Minor is one such example.[2] The inscription announces the "good news" of Caesar Augustus' birth as a god:

> Since Providence, which has ordered all things and is deeply interested in our life, has set in most perfect order by giving us

---

[2] See W. Dittenberger, *Orientis Graecae Inscriptiones Selectae*, trans. A.H. Jones, 2 vols (Leipzig: Hirzel, 1903-1905), II. 458.

Augustus, whom she filled with virtue that he might benefit humankind, sending him as a saviour both for us and for our descendants, that he might end war and arrange all things . . . and since the birth day of the god Augustus was the beginning of the good news for the world that came by reason of him . . .

The use of the imperial term "good news", together with Jewish traditions such as Second Isaiah's heralding of good tidings (Isaiah 40:9), provides the vehicle for Mark to announce the Good News of his own saviour. The phrase "Son of God" is missing from some of the earliest and best manuscripts and might be a later interpolation; its inclusion here, however, accords with Roman popular dedications to Augustus, such as the Priene inscription, which combine "beginning" and "good news" and "god". Ched Myers goes much further to argue that in the opening sentence, "Mark is taking dead aim at Caesar and his legitimising myths . . . It is a declaration of war upon the political culture of the empire." [3]

The identity of Jesus (his proper name) as Christos (an attribute) is central to understanding the distinctiveness of the protagonist as the anointed one. Jesus' identity as the Messiah explains why this story is Good News: we the readers are now privileged to know what few of the participants in the story will even guess. The "messianic secret" is a secret only from the other characters in the story. By announcing the identity of Jesus in the first sentence, Mark tells us how he wants us to read this story from the very beginning: everything we hear Jesus say and all that we see him do, his words and deeds, are revelatory of who he is. This is equally true of the other Gospels. Usually, in narrative, this works in reverse.

Normal storytelling	Gospel storytelling
a character's deeds and words,	reveals the main character's identity,
the impact he/she makes on us	provoking our interest from the beginning
provokes our interest	thus we interpret his deeds and words
so we become interested in the action	and appraise his impact on people

[3] C. Myers, *Binding the Strong Man: A Political Reading of Mark's Story of Jesus* (Maryknoll: Orbis Books, 1988), 122-124.

Everything we read about Jesus is interpreted inside Mark's opening disclosure of Jesus' identity; thus we will understand the significance of what Jesus does and says in a way the characters inside the story will not. They try to discover who Jesus is by interpreting his deeds and words ("Who is the man who...?"); they struggle to find meaning to their experience of Jesus, trying to uncover *what is going on* as they witness *what is actually happening*. For example, when the disciples are crossing the Sea of Galilee in a tempest and Jesus calms the waves and stills the storm, the disciples are moved to ask, "Who then is this, that even the wind and sea obey him?" (Mark 4:41). For Mark, what Jesus does provokes his disciples to wonder about his identity; it does not resolve that question. While the disciples of Jesus struggle with this, we the readers do not: that fundamental question has been resolved by the narrator in the opening sentence of his narrative.

The whole story Mark tells is only the beginning, ending with the empty tomb in 16:8 – the remainder of the story will be written by the community. Where is the beginning of the Jesus story? Where does that story have its origin?

The frame of Mark: the prophetic story

As some commentators have noted, the first two verses of Mark's Gospel may form a complete statement: "The beginning of the Gospel of Jesus Christ, the Son of God, as it is written in Isaiah the prophet..." Mark establishes the outer frame of the story in God's word of promise spoken to Israel: the evangelist builds a bridge back to the story of Israel not through a genealogy of ancestors but through the divine word. No upright Jew could accept the claims made about Jesus unless those claims were seen to be rooted in the Hebrew scriptures, the great narrative drama that outlines God's saving work. The mission of Jesus must be seen in conformity with Old Testament predictions. Thus Mark opens with the claim that the Jesus story is rooted in Israel's ancient prophetic word. Although there are quotations from the Old Testament made by other characters in Mark's Gospel, this is the only time Mark as narrator quotes scripture directly. Mark's quotation reads:

> Behold, I send my messenger before thy face,
> who shall prepare thy way;
> the voice of one crying in the wilderness:
> Prepare the way of the Lord,
> make his paths straight (Mark 1:2-3).

Mark's quotation seems a composite of Isaiah 40:3 and Malachi 3:1.

Isaiah 40:3
A voice cries: "In the wilderness
prepare the way of the Lord,
make straight in the desert a highway for our God."

Malachi 3:1
"Behold, I send my messenger to prepare the way before me, and the Lord whom you seek will suddenly come to his temple; the messenger of the covenant in whom you delight, behold, he is coming," says the Lord of hosts.

Clearly Mark did not have available to him the ancient scrolls of these texts: he was probably quoting from memory, cherishing the ancient promises of Isaiah about God's future salvation for the people. That promised salvation lay in the prophecies of Israel, particularly in the work of Isaiah. Although Second Isaiah (chapters 40-55) dates to the sixth century BC – probably written in Babylon in the 540s – Mark would have regarded Isaiah as a unified text dating back to the eighth-century prophet, Isaiah. Second Isaiah calls on his fellow exiles to leave Babylon, just as their ancestors had left Egypt, in a new exodus that would define them again as the people of Israel: the opening commission (Isaiah 40:1-11) is a proclamation of good news that God will restore Israel to Zion. This will be a triumphal procession through the wilderness, aiming for the true homeland of Zion, a great re-enactment of the exodus conquest; and God will provide water in the wilderness and rivers in the desert (43:20). As Isaiah called the people to a new journey through the wilderness to their true home, so John the Baptist will do the same.

Mark places the prophecy from Isaiah first and he then describes the appearance of John the Baptist. As Catherine Murphy comments:

> Both Matthew and Luke choose to place the prophecy from Isaiah 40:3 after the appearance of John, whereas Mark had placed it before John's manifestation in the desert. Mark's narrative placement conveys the sense of speed with which events unfold in the first chapters of his Gospel. Something is said, and immediately it occurs (though this word had been said many centuries before). In contrast, the relocation of an ancient prophecy after the present event has a more reflective quality, as if the evangelists were teaching the deeper meaning of, and divine plan behind, present events to their audiences.[4]

---

[4] C. Murphy, *John the Baptist: Prophet of Purity for a New Age* (Minnesota: Liturgical Press, 2003), 51.

Mark conveys more than a sense of speed: in asserting the divine plan first, which functions as his outer frame, he influences how the reader will interpret the events which he then narrates. After centuries of waiting on the promise, Mark's belief is that people will witness the fulfilment of that pledge in the ministry of John the Baptist and Jesus. The Jesus story does not happen out of the blue but as the fulfilment of ancient longings that were founded on God's word of promise. That word spoken by God to his chosen prophet Isaiah marks the real beginning of the Jesus story.

The quotation from prophecy focuses on two people, one who appears as the herald and the other whose arrival he announces. The two characters – no other characters are introduced in the prologue – will be identified as John the Baptist and Jesus. Mark does not locate the wilderness by offering any geographical details; it is the wilderness of the prophecy: the proclaimer will cry in the place designated in the prophecy. The central frame of the Jesus story, as in the other three Gospels, is set within the ministry of John the Baptist (see Table 2.1). Thus the breathless pace of Mark's Gospel begins in the midst of ongoing drama – as ancient prophecy and Israel's hopes are fulfilled, as John heralds an unknown follower, and as Jesus appears from obscurity to begin his prophetic mission.

The Isaian "way of the Lord" mapped out by Mark – a theme that some scholars argue dominates Mark's narrative[5] – leads from John's call to repentance, through Jesus' prophetic ministry announcing the Good News of the fulfilment of the ages, to his journey with his disciples up to Jerusalem and then back to Galilee. As John Riches comments:

> Mark's opening citation of "Isaiah the prophet" establishes from the outset a dialogue with the Isaianic notion of the way of the Lord, which leads from the desert to Zion. The Gospel starts in the wilderness with John and culminates in Jerusalem with the death of Jesus on the cross. But the way that is taken from the wilderness to Jerusalem is anything but straight, and the story does not end there.[6]

Certainly Mark will radically rework Isaiah's theme of restoration in which God restores to the people their land and sanctuary: Mark will replace the return to the land and sanctuary by the disciples' personal attachment to Jesus and their missionary action. Israel will be rejected and replaced by the new building of those who follow Christ, who is the cornerstone (Mark 12:10). Isaiah's way of the Lord leads no longer to the Temple: as the veil of the Temple is torn and the divine presence departs, a Gentile centurion will recognise in the dead Jesus the identity of the "son of God".

---

[5] See, for example, J. Marcus, *The Way of the Lord: Christological Exegesis of the Old Testament in the Gospel of Mark* (Edinburgh: T & T Clark, 1992); R. Watts, *Isaiah's New Exodus and Mark* (Tübingen: Mohr Siebeck, 1997).

[6] J. Riches, *Conflicting Mythologies: Identity Formation in the Gospels of Mark and Matthew* (Edinburgh: T & T Clark, 2000), 45.

Movement will eventually take the place of sacred *space*: the Temple will be destroyed and replaced by the new dynamic movement – "wherever the Gospel is preached in the whole world" (14:9). Notwithstanding Mark's creative reworking of Isaiah, the Isaian frame of Mark's story does provide theological continuity and visionary support to the emerging ministry of Jesus. The inner frame is thus defined by the outer frame; the continuity is secured when we meet three prophets in Mark's prologue in the persons of Isaiah, John the Baptist and Jesus. The prophetic proclamation of Isaiah is interpreted by Mark as being fulfilled in the ministry of John the Baptist. Jesus is introduced as an adult who leaves home, travelling south to connect with John in the wilderness of Judea. Isaiah's proclamation is fulfilled as John *proclaims*. Jesus will continue that prophetic story as he *proclaims* the kingdom of God (1:14). The word that was first announced by God to the prophet Isaiah is now seen in the present tense of the narrative, in the preaching of John and in the preaching of Jesus. Myers rightly summarises Mark's prologue in verses 1-15 as "a narrative of succession (Isaiah-John-Jesus-Kingdom)". [7]

As the outer frame focuses on the wilderness, so the inner frame begins there: *hē erēmos,* the wilderness, was the sprawling stage of a drama that was to define the people of Israel in the exodus from Egypt, the covenant with Moses at Sinai, the forty years of wandering before entrance into the Promised Land, and the return from exile in Babylon. In the exodus story the end of the wandering in the desert was marked by crossing the river Jordan, which acted as the threshold into a new life. Wilderness and river were the defining places in the journey. When Joshua led the people across the Jordan he was effectively leading a new people into the Promised Land. If John the Baptist is working mostly in Perea, part of the tetrachy of Herod Antipas – situated on the far side of the Jordan – the wilderness prophet is effectively sending back a renewed people from the wilderness, across the river Jordan, to the Promised Land. Flavius Josephus, the Jewish historian who eventually settled in Rome, underlines the charismatic and powerful influence that John the Baptist exercised on ordinary Jews when he writes:

> For Herod killed him, although he was a good man and bade the Jews to join in baptism, providing that they were cultivating virtue and practising justice towards one another and piety towards God . . . And when ordinary Jews gathered around John – for their excitement reached fever pitch as they listened to his words – Herod began to fear that John's powerful ability to persuade people might lead to some sort of revolt, for they seemed likely to do whatever he

---

[7] Myers, *Binding the Strong Man*, 122.

Table 2.1

THE FRAME OF MARK'S GOSPEL

The Prophetic Story

Frame: Back to proclamation, 8th cent BC: Isaiah
The Way of the Lord

The Public Ministry

John the Baptist *proclaims*

Jesus *proclaims*

End of the Gospel:
"and they (the women) said nothing to anyone,
for they were afraid." (16:8)

counselled. So Herod decided to do away with John first, before he sparked a revolt. Herod considered this a better course of action than to wait until the situation changed and then to regret his delay. And so, because of Herod's suspicion, John was sent in chains to Machaerus, the mountain fortress previously mentioned; there he was killed.[8]

Although Josephus makes no connection between John and Jesus, he underlines the authority of John to attract zealous adherence: according to his interpretation, Herod was threatened not only by John's persuasive speaking but by his awesome political power to spark a revolt. Herod's reported fear of John as an emerging political and military leader is an interesting counterbalance to the Gospels' tendency to neutralise the Baptist's independence and confine him inside the Christian story as the forerunner of the Messiah. Further, as Crossan comments: "Whatever John's intentions may have been, Antipas was not paranoid to consider a conjunction of prophet and crowds, desert and Jordan, dangerously volatile."[9]

In the opening poem, that Mark uses from Second Isaiah, the voice of God calls the prophet to prepare in the wilderness a way for God and to make a highway across the desert (Isaiah 40:3). It is interesting to note that this text was used by the Qumran community as one of the foundational texts to explain their presence in the desert of Judea – *Community Scroll* (1QS) 8:13-14; 9:19-20. Although Mark does not define the place (later specified by Matthew 3:1 as the desert of Judea), he notes that "all the country of Judea, and all the people of Jerusalem" went out to John (Mark 1:5). As the wilderness is the stage for the outer and inner frames of Mark's Gospel, it serves to connect the story of the people of Israel to the new story of Gospel: as the wilderness is the setting for forty years for the emergence of the people of Israel and the call of Isaiah to return from exile through the wilderness, so it is the setting for the ministry of John the Baptist, for Jesus' emergence from obscurity, and for his trial of forty days before the beginning of his ministry.

John the Baptist

Mark tells us very little about John – unlike Matthew and Luke he does not develop themes in John's preaching – and he shows no interest in the wilderness prophet for his own sake: Mark is writing the story of Jesus, so the material about John is clearly subordinated to Mark's overriding interest. As Joan Taylor comments:

[8] Flavius Josephus, *Antiquities*, 18.5.2.
[9] J.D. Crossan, *The Historical Jesus: The Life of a Mediterranean Jewish Peasant* (Edinburgh: T&T Clark, 1991), 232.

It is one thing to state that John would not be very significant historically if he had not had some contact with Jesus, but it is another thing to accept the Gospel's presentation of John, in which he is a kind of proto-Christian pointing the way to Jesus as Messiah. The Gospel writers wish us to believe that John really had no importance whatsoever in his own right and that his importance was entirely the result of witnessing to the arrival of the Messiah...

Since mention of John the Baptist in the New Testament is obviously overlaid with a developing insistence on Jesus' superiority, we can suppose that the issue of John himself was a problem for the early Church. Clearly John was not a nobody in his time, and the Gospels accord him respect. However, John was not permitted too much respect; people had to know his place. Most often the interpretations aim at neutralizing the Baptist's independence to make him safe for Christianity.[10]

By the time the Gospels are written, this wilderness prophet, who spearheaded a revival movement in Israel, has been domesticated within the Christian story and accorded his position as the forerunner to Jesus. It is worth noting that the writer of Acts records a situation in which some disciples of John seem unaware of Jesus' relationship to John (as did Flavius Josephus):

While Apollos was at Corinth, Paul passed through the upper country and came to Ephesus. There he found some disciples. And he said to them, "Did you receive the Holy Spirit when you believed?" And they said, "No, we have never even heard that there is a Holy Spirit." And he said, "Into what then were you baptised?" They said "Into John's baptism." And Paul said, "John baptised with the baptism of repentance, telling the people to believe in the one who was to come after him, that is, Jesus." On hearing this, they were baptised in the name of the Lord Jesus. And when Paul had laid his hands on them, the Holy Spirit came on them; and they spoke with tongues and prophesied (Acts 19:1-6).

This passage indicates that John's followers were still known as an independent group, and that they had spread to the Diaspora by the middle of the first century; further, it seems to suggest that John's preaching was not dependent on either the arrival of Jesus or a future spirit-immersion. Did they understand the coming baptism as an imminent baptism of fire? In the above passage Paul is seen to offer the

---

[10] J. Taylor, *John the Baptist within the Second Temple Judaism* (London: SPCK, 1997), 2,5.

standard Christian interpretation of John's message about the coming one, explaining the identity of this person, "that is, Jesus".

In Mark's Gospel John the Baptist does not recognise Jesus as the coming one, but clearly Mark does. The first character to appear onstage in Mark's drama is John the Baptist: his appearance heralds the beginning of the Jesus story. This is reflected in Peter's address to the centurion Cornelius: "You know the word which he sent to Israel, preaching Good News of peace by Jesus Christ (who is Lord of all), the word which was proclaimed thoughout all Judea, beginning from Galilee after the baptism which John preached." Peter's outline of the apostolic preaching (Acts 10:37-40) can be summarised thus:

a. **Following the preaching of John the Baptist**

b. **Jesus begins in Galilee**

c. **He is baptised/anointed with the Holy Spirit and power**

d. **Jesus travels around doing good and curing people**

e. **Those who were with him witnessed everything he did**

f. **in Judea and in Jerusalem**

g. **He was killed by hanging on a tree**

h. **On the third day God raised him to life**

i. **and allowed him to be seen.**

Apart from the last point, the resurrection appearances, Mark follows this outline programme faithfully. Jesus' beginning is firmly related to the preaching and person of John the Baptist. John appears on the stage of history *proclaiming* a baptism of repentance: baptism is not the subject of his preaching but the focus of his activity; John exercises the office of herald and proclaims his message with authority, summoning people to undergo his baptism.

John the Baptist's singular authority is illustrated in his ability to attract "all the country of Judea, and all the people of Jerusalem". Although Mark's statement is clearly hyperbolic, it is written to underline the unique drawing power of John's ministry. People are leaving sacred space in the city of Jerusalem – the holy city that is dominated by the Temple, the sacrificial system and the priests – and journeying into the profane space of the wilderness, to attend to a prophet's message. It seems a strange movement to open a Gospel – of a pilgrimage *away* from sacred space to a person who inhabits a wilderness that few would find attractive. The wilderness of Judea is a desert of stone not sand, where, at the time of

John, there would have been no fixed human habitation. The destination of the pilgrims, however, is not a place but a person: perhaps it is true to say that if people believe that someone speaks the word of God with authority, the geography of that person's surroundings becomes wholly irrelevant. That point is emphasised in Luke's account when Jesus asks the crowds the question: "What did you go out into the wilderness to behold?" (Luke 7:24).

The activity that characterises John the Baptist's ministry, as his name suggests, is his purifying rite with water. In Jewish tradition purity was a condition for approaching the divine presence, and many of the purity laws regulated access to the Temple. The worship of the God of Israel was localised in one place, the Temple, and the visitor to the Temple mount today can see the large immersion pools which pilgrims used for purification before entering the Temple precincts. While impurity could be incurred through natural bodily process and contact with unclean people or food – impurity was not a sin – the Law provided means of purification. As Paula Fredriksen writes: "A system of 'wash-and-wait' – immersion and observing a liminal time period (until sunset; seven days; forty days: it varied, depending on the case) – cleansed most impurities."[11] In the houses of rich Jews there was usually a *mikveh,* a ritual bath, plastered and chiselled into bedrock, for family use. Since the washing was to be done in living water rather than in drawn water, these ritual baths were filled with rainwater.

Purification through washing was a common practice among the Jews and there are some points of contact between John the Baptist, the hermit Bannus and the community at Qumran, all located in the Jordan valley and all mentioned by Flavius Josephus. Josephus, born in 37 BC, said that when he was nineteen years old he spent some time with an otherwise unknown hermit called Bannus. He described Bannus thus:

> He stayed in the wilderness, using cloth from trees, supporting himself by food that grows of itself, washing with cold water day and night frequently for sanctification, and I became his zealot.[12]

There are similarities with John the Baptist: living in the wilderness, the simplicity of clothing and diet, the presence of disciples, the washing for sanctification. The water rite of Bannus, however, like that of Qumran, is self-administered. The community of Qumran was made up probably of the most pious and strict sect of Essenes who exiled themselves from the city and the Temple, unlike those who lived in outlying villages or in a

[11] P. Fredriksen, *Jesus of Nazareth, King of the Jews* (London: Macmillan, 2000), 53.
[12] Josephus, *Life,* 2.11.

section of Jerusalem. They lived a monastic life in the wilderness of Judea not far from John's field of operation. While John and Qumran have points of contact – both believe Israel has gone astray; both believe in purification by water as a sign of repentance and renewed lives; both believe in a future of reckoning with God – there are substantial differences.

Candidates for admission to Qumran were required to be Jews and first undergo an initial scrutiny by the Guardian of the community, to assess their mental and moral stature. If they passed they were permitted to enter the Covenant of God in the presence of the whole community, vowing "by a binding oath to return with all his heart and soul to every commandment of the Law of Moses in accordance with all that has been revealed of it to the Sons of Zadok, the Keepers of the Covenant" (1QS 5:7-11). After another period receiving instruction from the Guardian the postulant would appear before the Congregation, who either accepted him as a novice or dismissed him. He was still not admitted to "purity" for another year. After the novitiate, the successful novice would be admitted to the daily baths of the community: according to the "Community Rule", however, there was no ritual of baptism that specifically marked entrance into the community itself; entrance was by the making of solemn vows.[13]

The water rituals at Qumran were self-administered: today you can see the excavations of two large ritual baths at either end of the complex, which would have provided opportunity for a large number of people to purify themselves – with separate steps for unclean descent and clean ascent. These ritual immersions were a daily practice and part of the life of a highly structured and exclusive community. As Hartmut Stegemann, director of the Qumran Research Centre at the University of Göttingen, observes in his excellent study:

> The Essenes prescribed these ritual purification procedures for each of their daily ritual gatherings, and instead of the cleansing only of hands, feet, and forehead, a ritual immersion of the entire body was required. That one first had to be physically clean was self-evident to the Essenes as well. The performance of the baths of immersion was a ritual obligation, not a bodily cleansing, nor did it have anything to do with the forgiveness of sins.[14]

[13] But see G. Vermes, *The Dead Sea Scrolls in English* (Harmondsworth: Penguin, 1965), 45 which interprets 1QS 3 to read that there was a purificatory rite of entrance into the Covenant: "This seems to have been a peculiar and solemn act similar to Christian baptism . . ."

[14] H. Stegemann, *The Library of Qumran: On the Essenes, Qumran, John the Baptist, and Jesus* (Leiden: Brill, 1998), 192.

John the Baptist, by comparison, is a solitary nomadic prophet and sole administrator of his water ritual; the one-time character of John's baptism is the exact opposite of the Essene practice; John's baptism was directly related to the Last Judgement and the forgiveness of sins; John does not demand his converts to join an exclusive settled community with him at its head. Further, while he has disciples, he aims his ministry at all Jews, including the marginalised, who then return to their normal lives after baptism in the Jordan. In Qumran the Essenes admitted to their immersions only full members of the community, who had undergone a probationary period; John baptises all who come to him, without any period of waiting. In his ministry John makes himself available to all the people, offering them opportunities for repentance and forgiveness, rather than withdrawing to an elite community of believers focused on its own sanctification.

Mark describes John the Baptist in language that closely parallels a description of Elijah at the river Jordan in 2 Kings 1:8. In popular Jewish tradition – see Malachi 4:5-6 – Elijah was expected to return to announce the arrival of the Messiah. Later in the narrative Jesus will affirm that John is indeed Elijah (Mark 9:13). John wears an outer garment of camel hair – clothing commonly used by Bedouin to protect them from the heat of the day and the cold of the night – held by a leather belt. His normal diet of locusts and honey from wild bees would reflect not only an ascetic lifestyle but, perhaps more immediately, the scarcity of food that was available to desert nomads.

While ritual impurity was not a sin and could be overcome with washing, sin normally required sacrifices and offerings. John's water ritual is radically different, however, being "a baptism of repentance for the forgiveness of sins" (Mark 1:4). The Greek verb *baptizein* means to dip, plunge, or immerse: John is unique because he administers his water ritual himself, plunging people into the living waters of the Jordan. When people are baptised by him, they confess their sins to John. This appears strange, since forgiveness of sins in most religious traditions, including Judaism at the time, was mediated by priests, whereas John the Baptist is a lay prophet. Before Titus and the tenth legion turned the Temple into a heap of smouldering ruins in AD 70, the sacred place was the centre of elaborate ritual and customs, many focusing on forgiveness and atonement. The means for making gift offerings, bringing agricultural produce, burning incense, and sacrificing animals (pigeons and doves, lambs, goats and rams, and finally bulls) was elaborately laid down. In the sacrifice of animals, the priest, on behalf of the petitioner, offered gifts to God or else paid for a sin, redeeming it: at the heart of this priestly sacrifice was the acknowledgement and confession of sin by the petitioner and the understanding that God desires to forgive and will forgive the sinner seeking forgiveness. The Temple, after all, was believed to be the cosmic centre of the universe, the place where heaven and earth converged, the place of God's presence among humanity.

The pilgrimage from Jerusalem into the wilderness dramatises a shift: the confession of sins and forgiveness are now moving away from sacred space and priestly hands and sacrificial altar to the person of John, who mediates the forgiveness of God. God's forgiving presence is moving out of the sanctuary. Interestingly Flavius Josephus, describing the destruction of the Temple by fire, speaks of an earlier revelation in the Temple: "And upon the feast day called Pentecost, at night the priests going into the inner Temple to offer their wonted sacrifice, at first felt the place to move and tremble, and afterwards they heard a voice which said, let us depart hence."[15] In this scene the God of Israel, announcing his departure, tells his people that from then onwards he would not allow walls built with stone to enclose him.

John the Baptist dramatically anticipates this scene: the God of Israel is at work through John's ministry in the wilderness, in the open air, in non-sacred space. God's work will continue in the one who is to come after John, who will also mediate God's forgiveness. While most prophets recall people to fidelity to the covenant, John the Baptist points forwards not backwards, to an unidentified mightier one who will come after him. This stronger one, whose sandals the wilderness prophet is unworthy to untie, will also be a baptiser like John – the marked difference being that his baptism will be with the Holy Spirit rather than with water.

John is not only the precursor of Jesus: in the wilderness, in his ministry of preaching, in his nomadic lifestyle, in calling Israel to repentance, in attracting large crowds of people, and in his forgiveness of sins, but also a dramatic precursor in his violent death. As John died at the hands of a hesitant king – even though Herod knew him to be "a righteous and holy man" (Mark 6:20) – so Jesus will die at the hands of an ambivalent governor who asks, "Why? What evil has he done?" (Mark 15:14). The career of both these resolute men will reach a climax in their execution at the hands of vacillating civil authorities. To know of John is to know in advance of Jesus.

---

[15] Josephus, *Jewish War*, 6. See also Tacitus, *History*, 5.13.

Jesus is baptised

"In those days Jesus came from Nazareth of Galilee and was baptised by John in the Jordan" (Mark 1:9). As the Baptist is seen to fulfil the ancient prophecies of preparing a way for the Lord, the first image of Jesus is the traveller on the way. Throughout Mark's Gospel he will remain a traveller on the way, constantly moving from place to place, until he reaches his objective in Jerusalem. For Mark, Jesus' whole public ministry is a journey: the country prophet from the Galilean village of Nazareth will make his way eventually to the southern city of Jerusalem. The city of his destination will define his destiny.

Mark has no birth stories and he never mentions Bethlehem or Joseph in his narrative. He introduces an adult Jesus who comes from a village so small that it needs further identification, "of Galilee". Jesus' journey follows a personal decision to leave home and make the four-day journey south to be baptised by John – the passive voice indicates John as the main agent. When Jesus comes to John there is no recognition scene: John does not know what we the readers know. Rather than witness John baptising Jesus, the reader is made to look heavenwards, to witness three wonderful elements denied to others: as Jesus emerges from the water, he sees the heavens open; he sees the Spirit descend; he hears the heavenly voice address him personally, identifying him as God's Son (see Psalm 2:7; Isaiah 42:1).

The baptism of Jesus by John – there is no narrative detail of this event – is completely overshadowed by the theophany. Our attention is diverted away from seeing Jesus submit to John – an embarrassing image of *the mightier one* submitting in a baptism for the forgiveness of sins *to the forerunner* – to witnessing what Jesus sees and hears of God's revealing activity. God, not John, becomes the main agent in the story. Suddenly the local scene at the river Jordan has become a cosmic stage, effectively shifting attention away from John's baptism of water to a Christian baptism in the Spirit. Now the voice of God, not the voice of the evangelist, announces to the reader the true identity of Jesus.

There are two distinct elements to the baptism story: the simple element of what actually happens as Jesus leaves home and travels south to be baptised by John in the river Jordan and the wonderful element that interprets what is going in the heavens opening, the Spirit's descending, and the heavenly voice addressing Jesus. Through both elements, the simple and the wonderful, the evangelists combine experience and meaning, fact and interpretation, event and significance. The wonderful element interprets *for the readers* the significance of the baptism of Jesus. If the wonderful element was available to other witnesses at the river Jordan, why does nobody in the Gospel narrative ever mention it when people speak about Jesus' identity?

Table 2.2

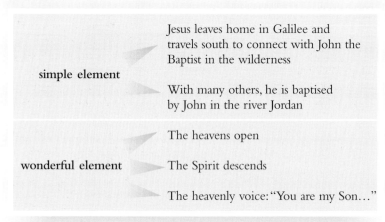

simple element	Jesus leaves home in Galilee and travels south to connect with John the Baptist in the wilderness
	With many others, he is baptised by John in the river Jordan
wonderful element	The heavens open
	The Spirit descends
	The heavenly voice: "You are my Son…"

In the wonderful element the focus now dramatically shifts away from John the Baptist: God and his Spirit are now the main actors; Jesus is still the recipient. Mark uses a selection of Old Testament texts to bring out the meaning of the baptism of Jesus. Again the influence of Isaiah prevails:

Psalm 2:7 I will tell of the decree of the Lord:
He said to me, "You are my son,
today I have begotten you."

Isaiah 42:1 Behold my servant, whom I uphold,
my chosen, in whom my soul delights;
I have put my Spirit upon him,
he will bring forth justice to the nations.

Isaiah 63:7–64:12: *The Prayer of Israel*
…Where is the one who brought them up out of the sea
with the shepherds of his flock?
Where is the one who put within them his holy spirit?…
Look down from heaven and see,
from your holy and glorious habitation . . .

> For you are our father . . .
> our Redeemer from of old is your name . . .
> O that you would tear open the heavens and come down...
> ...to make your name known to your adversaries . . .
> Zion has become a wilderness, Jerusalem a desolation ...
> Will you keep silent, and punish us so severely?

The wonderful element successfully removes the embarrassment of the simple element, diverting attention away from John the Baptist's role and focusing on Jesus as the anointed Son of God. Writing earlier than Mark, Paul speaks of the *resurrection* as the moment Jesus is designated Son of God (Romans 1:4). Likewise in presenting the preaching of Peter and Paul in Acts, Luke has Peter argue that in raising Jesus from the dead "God has made him both Lord and Christ this Jesus whom you crucified" (Acts 2:36); in the same way, Luke has Paul share the understanding that in raising Jesus from the dead, the Davidic enthronement psalm is fulfilled: "You are my son, today I have begotten you" (Psalm 2:7; Acts 13:33). Mark now applies this psalm, together with Isaiah's texts, to the baptism of Jesus. Further, the prayer of Israel in Isaiah can be considered answered in the baptism scene: the heavens *are* torn open, the Holy Spirit of God *is* sent down; God's silence *is broken* as he now speaks, revealing the identity of his Son. Thus interpreted, the baptism of Jesus is not an individual event, but is interpreted as the answer to the longings of Israel.

The wonderful element fulfils the function of clarifying the identity and mission of Jesus, at the same time asserting the importance of Jesus over John the Baptist. The wonderful element, however, is not to be read in the same light as the simple element. As John P. Meier argues: "The theophany does not mirror some inner experience Jesus had at the time; it mirrors the desire of the first-generation Christian church to define Jesus as soon as the primitive Gospel story begins – all the more so because this definition was needed to counter the impression of Jesus' subordination to John, implicit in the tradition of the former being baptized by the latter."[16]

There is obvious nervousness shared by the four evangelists, evident in their writing about John and Jesus, and it is worth noting how they handle the embarrassing memory of Jesus becoming a convert of John the Baptist through submitting to his rite of purification:

Mark admits it – saying that Jesus is baptised by John in the Jordan, but he narrates no detail of this event, shifting attention away from John's

---

[16] J.P. Meier, *A Marginal Jew: Rethinking the Historical Jesus, II: Mentor, Message and Miracles* (New York: Doubleday, 1994), 107.

baptism to the theophany witnessed by Jesus (and the reader): when Jesus comes out of the water, he sees the heavens open and the Spirit descending on him. The heavenly voice speaks directly to Jesus: "You are my beloved Son . . ."

Matthew explains it – since he is clearly worried that the baptism scene might create misunderstanding, resulting in his readers seeing Jesus as both subordinate to John and sinful. Matthew has John recognise Jesus when he comes for baptism; John demurs, saying that the roles should be reversed since he needs baptism from Jesus. Only after Jesus reassures John and gives him permission does John proceed. The heavenly voice now declares: "This is my Son . . ." (Matthew 3:17).

Luke hides it – telling the story of John's imprisonment first, he then states that Jesus is baptised without mentioning the name of the baptiser. Luke shifts the wonderful elements away from the baptism scene to a prayer experience of Jesus: "After Jesus was baptised, and while he was at prayer, the heavens opened . . ." (Luke 3:21-22). The heavenly voice, as in Mark's account, addresses Jesus directly.

John suppresses it – never mentioning the baptism of Jesus. John retains the wonderful element of the Spirit descending like a dove: this revelation is addressed to John not Jesus, the opposite of the Markan text. Given the fourth evangelist's theology and the language of his prologue, he is not having the eternal *Logos* (the word that is God) submit to *anthrōpos* (the man who came sent by God as a witness to speak for the light).[17]

However the baptism of Jesus is understood, what does become clear is that while Jesus is with John he makes a decision to change his life. After his time with John the Baptist, and we cannot be clear about how long this period lasts, Jesus follows John in living the life of a nomadic prophet and preaching the need for repentance: indeed so alike are they that Herod agrees with the most popular theory about Jesus' identity, that Jesus is John the Baptist, raised from the dead (Mark 6:16). Further, when Jesus asks his disciples who people say he is, the dominant view reported back to him is that he is John the Baptist (Mark 8:28). Clearly these two prophets are perceived to be very alike.

In making a decision to change his life, Jesus becomes more like John. The measure of that life change will be indicated by Mark later in the narrative when he notes that when Jesus returns home, "[his family] went out to restrain him, for people were saying, 'He has gone out of his mind'" (Mark 3:21). And when Jesus returns to Nazareth, to teach in the

---

[17] The evangelist John has no story either of the baptism of Jesus or the transfiguration of Jesus, both events focusing on the identity of Jesus as God's Son.

synagogue, the negative reaction of his own townspeople is noted: "Where did this man get all this? What is this wisdom given to him?... Is not this the carpenter, the son of Mary... And they took offence at him" (6:2-3). This disparaging reaction leads Jesus to share his belief that a prophet is despised among his own people and in his own house. So negative is the whole experience that it renders Jesus almost powerless and amazed at their lack of faith (6:6). The Jesus who returns to Nazareth after his time with John is clearly perceived by those who know him as radically different from the Jesus who lived there before setting eyes on John. That difference indicates a clear life change made by Jesus, one that Jesus lives out until his death, and Mark's narrative indicates that Jesus decided upon this option while he was with John the Baptist.

Jesus is tempted by Satan

Immediately following the baptism scene, Mark tells the story of Jesus being tempted by Satan, a brief account that Joachim Jeremias calls "astonishingly obscure. It consists of statements which bear the stamp of symbolic biblical language".[18] Both Matthew (4:1-11) and Luke (4:1-13) narrate a series of three temptations against a background of texts from Deuteronomy that explore Israel's ordeal in the wilderness. Mark has no mention of fasting or hunger; no mention of the nature of the struggles; no mention of the outcome. All we know is that the Spirit does not protect Jesus from trial, but projects him to the place of ambiguity where he must reckon with Satan.

The Spirit propels (*ekballei*) Jesus into the wilderness, a verb suggesting that the Spirit has taken possession of Jesus as his driving force. The Spirit is the principal actor – Jesus himself is not named in Mark's account of the temptation. It is worth noting again that after Jesus' baptism by John, the ground shifts dramatically: we the readers are suddenly standing on a cosmic stage with the heavens opening, the Spirit descending, and the voice of God speaking. Although the wilderness is mentioned for the third time as the geographical setting of the action, the cosmic stage is still set as the Spirit drives Jesus into the wilderness to be confronted by Satan.

The ultimate significance of Jesus is measured by a larger stage than regional geography can provide: this is not a local debate between two human combatants, but a cosmic struggle between good and evil, between the Son of God and Satan. There is no human actor on this stage apart from Jesus himself. The temptation by Satan sets the stage of elemental

---

[18] J. Jeremias, *New Testament Theology, I: The Proclamation of Jesus* (London: SCM, 1972), 69.

conflict for the defeat of the power of evil, although Mark does not tell us the outcome of the encounter. Later, however, the evangelist will show Jesus describing his ministry of exorcism as binding the powerful Satan and robbing Satan of his spoil (3:22-30).

The cosmic stage – seen by the readers but by no other character in the Gospel – is denoted by the presence of wild beasts and angels. Angelic guardians and wild beasts are also found in Psalm 91:11-13:

> On their hands they will bear you up,
> so that you will not dash your foot against a stone.
> You will tread on the lion and the adder,
> the young lion and the serpent you will trample under foot.

Exodus 23:20 also contains a ministering angel:

> Behold, I send an angel before you, to guard you on the way and to bring you to the place which I have prepared.

With the coming of the Messiah all animals will live in harmony, a picture celebrated in Isaiah's messianic poem which describes the principal characteristics of the coming Messiah, the one who will be filled with the spirit of the prophets and who will restore the peace of paradise:

> The wolf shall dwell with the lamb,
>   and the leopard shall lie down with the kid,
> and the calf and the lion and the fatling together,
>   and a little child shall lead them.
> The cow and the bear shall feed;
>   their young shall lie down together;
>   and the lion shall eat straw like the ox.
> The sucking child shall play over the hole of the asp,
>   and the weaned child shall put his hand on the adder's den.
> They shall not hurt or destroy
>   in all my holy mountain;
> for the earth shall be full of the knowledge of the Lord
>   as the waters cover the sea (Isaiah 11:6-9).

As the word of God addressed to Isaiah forms the outer frame of Mark's Gospel, and as the inner frame is set in the wilderness of Isaiah's prophecy, so Isaiah's dream of restoration is realised in the coming of Jesus. It is an image of paradise regained. Dale Allison goes further and argues that Mark's temptation scene is a dramatic reversal of the sequence of the paradise story in Genesis:

> In paradise Adam lived in peace with the animals and was guarded and/or honoured by angels. There too he was fed by angels or (according to another tradition) ate the food of angels, manna. But after succumbing to the temptation of the serpent he was cast out (the verb is *ekebalon* in Gen 3:24 LXX).

> This sequence of events is turned upside down in Mark. Jesus is first cast out. Then he is tempted. Then he gains companionship with the animals and the service of angels.[19]

Certainly the story is weighted with pre-history. In not developing the temptations by Satan into a narrative, however, Mark leaves us with the dominant image not of how Satan tempts Jesus but of how Jesus inhabits the wilderness. If the wilderness is the scene, paradise is the dream earthed in the Messiah being with the wild beasts while the angels minister to him.

Jesus begins his ministry

While some scholars argue that Mark 1:1-13 forms the prologue to his Gospel, others argue for the prologue to include verses 14-15, marking the beginning of Jesus' ministry of preaching the kingdom of God. While Mark in verse 1 announces the beginning of the Gospel, there is a sense in which that beginning is marked by the preaching of Jesus. As Scaria Kuthirakkattel notes: "Mark 1:14-15 complements not only the title of the book (1:1) but rounds out the whole introduction in such a way that the entire fifteen verses stand as a genuine prologue to the whole subsequent text."[20]

Mark dates the beginning of Jesus' ministry with the notice of John the Baptist's arrest. With the messianic forerunner now offstage permanently – Mark delays the details of his death until a narrative flashback in chapter 6 – the Messiah now steps onto the stage as an active agent. No longer do things happen to him – being baptised in the Jordan, being driven by the Spirit into the wilderness, being tempted by Satan – but he is seen, in the active voice, to make things happen as he goes into Galilee and proclaims the Gospel of God. And just as John was handed over (*paradothenai*), this same verb will be used twenty times by Mark, usually to indicate the

---

[19] D. Allison, "Behind the Temptations of Jesus: Q 4:1-13 and Mark 1:12-13", in B.D. Chilton and C.A. Evans (eds), *Authenticating the Activities of Jesus* (Leiden: Brill, 1999), 187-188.

[20] S. Kuthirakkattel, *The Beginning of Jesus' Ministry According to Mark's Gospel (1:14-3:6): A Redaction Critical Study* (Analecta Biblica, 123; Rome: Pontifical Biblical Institute, 1990), 4.

violent fate that will befall Jesus in his passion and death, and to summarise a similar fate facing Jesus' own disciples (e.g. 9:31; 10:33; 13:11; 14:10; 15:10).

Although Jesus is from Galilee, Mark does not say that he returns there but, more purposefully, that Jesus went into Galilee (1:14). Going into Galilee denotes the formal beginning of Jesus' public ministry, and there he proclaims Good News from God. Given the key role Isaiah has played in Mark's prologue, it is not surprising that the prophet's influence is present in Mark's text to the end of the introduction. Isaiah predicts that the Davidic Messiah will honour Galilee in the future. The following few lines in prose introduce the poetic oracle of First Isaiah that celebrates the epiphany of the Messiah: gloom will be banished and Galilee will be honoured:

> But there will be no gloom for those who were in anguish. In the former time he brought into contempt the land of Zebulun and the land of Naphtali, but in the latter time he will make glorious the way of the sea, the land beyond the Jordan, Galilee of the nations (Isaiah 9:1).

Isaiah's subsequent oracle provides Mark with additional motivation to place Jesus' formal beginning in Galilee. In Mark 1:14-15 the writing forms a programmatic statement that sums up the basic purpose of the public ministry. Mark opened his Gospel by introducing us to John the Baptist and honouring the unique role John played in the story of Jesus' beginning. Now Mark tells us that Jesus' beginning in Galilee is directly related to the arrest of John: after John is handed over, Jesus' ministry begins. Both Matthew and Luke follow Mark, consciously excluding John from the time of Jesus' ministry. This avoids anything that looks like rivalry between the two major actors; instead, Jesus is presented as John's successor.

Whereas John proclaimed the one who was to come after him, Jesus proclaims "the Gospel of God" (1:14) – a phrase that serves as a standard Christian designation for the post-Easter proclamation about Jesus, beginning with John the Baptist and concluding with the death and resurrection of Jesus. Using the term here, Mark clearly wants to root the whole Gospel in the preaching of Jesus himself. Thus Mark assimilates "the Good News of Jesus Christ" (1:1) that he is proclaiming in writing with the Good News of God that Jesus announces in his ministry.

Although the kingdom of God forms the centre of Jesus' teaching, he never defines it and he is never asked to explain it to his hearers. The assumption is that his hearers knew what he meant, that it was a common term in their thinking vocabulary. As Geza Vermes notes: "By the time Jesus first meditated on it, the idea of the Kingdom of God had already a lengthy history in the Hebrew Bible and in early post-biblical or inter-testamental literature."[21] Although the *idea* has a lengthy history, the phrase "kingdom of God" appears only once in the Old Testament (Wisdom 10:10): as an expression it is basically a New Testament one, yet Jesus took it for granted that his listeners could catch its meaning.

The term "kingdom of God" yields a variety of interpretations which scholars have attempted to harmonise – not least whether it is "present" or "future" or both. The ambiguity is rooted in the Synoptic Gospels themselves where Jesus speaks of the kingdom as both future and present. When Jesus is referring to the final vindication of God's purposes, clearly this kingdom is in the future. When Jesus is referring to the sovereign rule of God in the world, this reality is not only in the future but present in Jesus' ministry of forgiveness and healing and exorcism. Norman Perrin refers to the kingdom of God as a "tensive symbol"[22] – one that does not have a single defined meaning but a whole range of meanings that defies neat definition. In this understanding, it is storytelling, metaphors, sayings and parables that will illustrate the different meanings of the kingdom of God as the Gospel proceeds.

The kingdom of God lies in the immediate future: God's kingly rule has drawn near, but it will not be long before people experience its power in the deeds and words of Jesus. Before that happens, Jesus makes the imperative appeal that is clearly addressed to all the hearers/readers of the Gospel: "Repent, and believe in the Good News."

If the kingdom is what God brings close, if the Good News is what Jesus proclaims, repenting and believing are the appropriate human responses we make. As hearers of the Gospel we are not passive note-takers of an abstruse lecture, but people challenged to do something about our own lives and become engaged in an adventure of radical change. The verb "repent" (*metanoeō*) literally means to think beyond the way we think now, to change our minds. That change involves taking to heart the Good News of God in Jesus, believing the message of the Gospel. The prologue of Mark is thus rounded off with the same term as it began, framed by the "Good News".

[21] G. Vermes, *The Religion of Jesus the Jew* (London: SCM, 1993), 121.

[22] N. Perrin, *Jesus and the Language of the Kingdom* (Philadelphia: Fortress, 1976), 29ff.

Conclusion

With the beginning of Jesus' ministry, we the readers are able to interpret the ensuing drama in the light of what we have learned in the prologue, theological insights that are not given to the participants in the Gospel story. While Jesus is alive, no human being in Mark's Gospel understands his true identity. From the prologue we know that the story we are about to hear is good news for which Israel and the prophets have been waiting for long. We have learned that the ministry of John the Baptist and Jesus is the fulfilment of an ancient word spoken to Isaiah, and that the message proclaimed by John and Jesus is in profound sympathetic continuity with the prophetic witness of Israel, setting out "the way of the Lord".

We have heard both the evangelist's and God's proclamation of Jesus' identity; we have learned that Jesus' baptism can be properly interpreted as an answer to the profound yearnings expressed in the Prayer of Israel – a new age has dawned because now the heavens have opened, the Spirit has descended, and God's voice has spoken. We have seen that Jesus moves in the power of the Spirit and that, although he is tempted by Satan, he enshrines the Isaian dream of paradise regained: in him God's original order in creation is restored. By the conclusion of the prologue, we have heard not only who Jesus is but what his mission is, that he proclaims the Good News of God, announcing the kingdom is close, and calling everyone to a change of heart. These insights make us companions in faith with Mark as we prepare to follow the great narrative of Jesus' public ministry and death.

When Jesus begins his ministry no one knows who he is; we, however, do know that he is the Christ and Son of God, in the light of what we have learned from the prologue. While Peter will confess that Jesus is the Christ, he is given strict orders to tell no one – a confession that is qualified by Peter's misunderstanding that earns him the rebuke, "Get behind me, Satan! For you are setting your mind not on divine things but on human things" (Mark 8:33). Only at the end of Mark's story is Jesus openly proclaimed as Messiah, in the title above the cross; only on the cross is he acknowledged as God's Son, and this singular acknowledgement by a human being in the Gospel is made not by a disciple but by a Gentile centurion.

The prologue declares unambiguously who Jesus is; the remainder of the Gospel, however, will show different people reacting to Jesus with incomprehension, incredulity and obstinacy, culminating in the aggressive will of the religious authorities to kill him. We might find it difficult to understand, reading the remainder of the Gospel, why disciples and enemies alike do not grasp the truth of Jesus' identity, why only the demons seem to know who he is, why so many people wonder whether he is working for God or Satan, why there is such a growing hostility to this man whose message is Good News. Why can't they see what we see? Why does his own family believe him to be out of his mind? Why, astonished as some are by the authority of Jesus, can't they answer their own question, "Who is this man?"

The characters in the Gospel cannot see what we see because they are in a drama without a prologue. It is not that we are bright and they are dim-witted; or that we are believers and they are not. As readers of the Gospel we enjoy a critical advantage over the participants in the Gospel drama: we have a teacher in Mark who has carefully set the stage for us, who has identified the protagonist and explained his mission. We read the story in the light of our guide's understanding, which he shares with us in his introduction.

The only other human being to appear as a character in the prologue is John the Baptist and he is arrested and off the scene by the time Jesus begins his ministry. We the readers are the only remaining witnesses; nobody knows what has been given to us to know. We have been given the secret that makes sense of all that is to come. Thanks to Mark.

3 The beginning of Matthew

Introduction

Matthew wrote his Gospel around AD 80 for a mainly Jewish-Christian audience, probably in Antioch, Syria, one of the four great centres of learning in the ancient world. From the internal structure and argument of the Gospel it would appear that Matthew's community starts its life as a Jewish-Christian group, affirming its Jewish roots, but ends up seeing itself as separate from its parent group, coming into open conflict with official Judaism, which now regards it as a deviant group.[1] Matthew's community, after much struggle, has also come to terms with the influx of Gentiles. Sectarian in nature, the community is marginalised not only from official Judaism but from the wider world that is dominated by the power of Rome. Prior to the destruction of the Temple, relations between Judaism and Christianity were relatively peaceful: the conflict with Judaism follows the sacking of Jerusalem and the consequent realignment of the Jewish people in the light of this catastrophic event. The end of the Temple marks the end of an era for both Jews and Christians.

No other building in the ancient world has commanded so much attention through the ages as the Temple in Jerusalem. Apart from the seventy years of desolation in the wake of the Babylonian conquest of Jerusalem, the influence of the Temple lasted a millennium: from the origins of the monarchy in the tenth century BC, when it was constructed by King Solomon, until the capture of Jerusalem in AD 70, when Titus and the tenth legion left the whole of the Temple mount in smouldering ruins. During the millennium of its influence the Temple played not only a central religious and cultic role in Israelite life, but it also functioned at a political level, from its origins as a state institution which gave legitimacy to the monarchy until its destruction by the Romans as the unifying symbol of Jewish identity.

The basic term for the Temple was *bêt Yahweh or bêt 'ĕlōhîm* – "house of Yahweh" or "house of God" – the word "house" stressing its residential nature as the divine dwelling-place on earth. Although the God of Israel was viewed as a transcendent being, the need for the nearness and protection of the divine power led the people of Israel to establish a place in which access to the transcendent God could be secured. The elaborate and costly furnishings were an indication of the building's occupant, with the glory of those furnishings signifying the Glory within.

---

[1] For a discussion that sees Matthew's community as a deviant sect *within* Judaism, see A. Saladrini, *Matthew's Christian-Jewish Community* (Chicago: University of Chicago Press, 1994).

The Temple as moral centre was symbolised by the physical presence of the two tablets of stone contained in the ark, on which were written the moral imperatives of the Israelite covenant with God. The Holy of Holies symbolised not only the divine presence of God among his people but also the establishment of social order through the Law. At the heart of the most sacred place in the Temple, which was the most sacred place in Judaism, was the Law.

By the time Matthew writes his Gospel, Judaism has undergone devastating change with the plunder and destruction of the Temple as part of Rome's suppression of the Jewish Revolt (AD 66-73). In the Catholic Christian world, if St Peter's Basilica in Rome were destroyed, that loss would be felt throughout the Catholic world; but the destruction would not mark the end of cultic worship and priesthood. The Temple, however, was radically different because it functioned as the only place of worship in the Jewish world. As Simon Goldhill comments:

> According to the Book of Kings, King Hezekiah and then, most successfully, King Josiah demanded the abolition of all cultic activity throughout the kingdom outside Jerusalem, and a restriction of all religious services to the Temple in Jerusalem. There were many religious sites in Judah and Israel, shrines like Shiloh, where the Ark had been kept for years, pillars where Jews worshipped and altars of sacrifice. According to the Book of Kings all of these were to be destroyed, along with all vestiges of local cult . . . All Jews in Judah and Israel had to come to Jerusalem to worship, especially on the three pilgrim festivals of Passover, Tabernacles, and Pentecost.[2]

The Temple became the one and only sacred centre for worship. While this centralisation effectively gave the Temple immense power, also positioning the priesthood at the centre of command and control, it also created a unique weakness: what would happen to worship and priesthood if the Temple were destroyed? Following its destruction by fire, the sacred place of worship was wasted and, as a consequence, the high priestly families were disempowered and the priesthood itself became superfluous overnight: Judaism would now rely on rabbinic leadership. Brutal events had changed everything; history had moved on; the unifying religious symbol of Israel had gone up in flames; Jews had suffered a series of devastating blows to their pride and self-consciousness, which would be exacerbated by their depiction in chains on coinage throughout the Roman Empire.

---

[2] S. Goldhill, *The Temple of Jerusalem* (London: Profile Books, 2004), 24.

In order to survive as a community, the Jews had to seek new ways of sustaining their sense of identity, forge new institutions and discover new patterns of religious identity – while still maintaining a sense of continuity with the past. Judaism was forced to redefine itself: who are you when the focal point of your identity has been destroyed?

The Pharisees, under the leadership of Yohanan ben Zakkai, set up a Sanhedrin in the coastal town of Jamnia, to reorganise Judaism without Temple and priesthood. These leaders were concerned with the disunity of the Jewish people and with the attraction of new movements, such as Christianity. To promote their own unity, strict demarcations eventually ensued, excluding other groups seen as endangering the identity of the Jewish religion; the process was begun of collecting their oral laws, establishing a standard calendar, and transferring to the synagogue rites that were previously performed in the Temple. The old tolerance for religious diversity was evaporating: the synagogue would replace the Temple, and the Hebrew scripture would become the focal point of Jewish identity, together with strict adherence to the Law as interpreted by the rabbis. Jewish-Christians began to be excluded from their parent religion because they venerated Jesus as Messiah, they were not strict followers of Torah, and they had begun to show a new openness to Gentile influence.

Christians are now becoming excluded from the synagogue: Matthew speaks of Jesus preaching in "*their* synagogues" (4:23; 9:35; 10:17; 12:9; 13:54; 23:34) – transposing back to the time of Jesus the break in Matthew's own time. Fierce arguments develop with the Pharisees, which are projected back into the Gospels – see, for example, the whole of chapter 23. As part of this new religious landscape, Matthew writes his Gospel:

  to create for the Christian community a sense of its own group identity

  to offer a new interpretation of Jewish tradition and salvation history

  to present a new way of looking at Christ

  to defend the Christian faith against Jewish accusations

  to open up the mission to the Gentiles.

As history had moved on, so Matthew does the same: he does not settle into theological nostalgia, regretting the passing of the good old days, but faces this time of turbulence and transition with new vigour. To those in his community who regarded themselves as Jewish-Christians and have now been expelled from their parent group, he offers a new community and a new identity. Matthew is the only evangelist to use the word *ekklēsia* – "assembly" or "Church" – in his writing (see 16:18; 18:17); this *ekklēsia* is the new community that is founded on Peter's confession of Jesus as the Messiah. The reason Jewish-Christians are expelled from the synagogue – for professing Jesus as the Christ – is the very foundation stone of the new community.

Matthew will reverence the tradition but he will inaugurate the new. In Matthew's thinking it is not true to make the generalisation that Jews rejected Jesus: Jesus himself and all of his first followers were Jews, who lived in deep respect of the tradition. It is later Rabbinic Judaism that rejects the identity of Jesus as Messiah – hence Christian leaders must not be called "rabbi" (23:7-8). The evangelist opens his Gospel by securing the Jewish identity of Jesus in the genealogy. While the genealogy celebrates Jesus' Jewish roots, by the end of the Gospel story the focus is shifting outwards to the Gentile world: the risen Jesus commissions his disciples to go and preach to all nations and teach them "to observe all that I have commanded you" (28:20). Matthew returns to the image of Jesus as the great teacher, the new development being that the Jewish teacher now opens up his teaching to the waiting world. And the initiation into this community is not circumcision but baptism.

What Matthew is trying to do is to portray Jesus as a true Israelite, one who is totally loyal to the tradition, and one whose coming has been announced in ancient prophecy. As Paula Fredriksen writes: "By viewing scripture primarily as a collection of prophecies awaiting fulfilment, Matthew could implicitly expose the incompleteness of Judaism. Only Jesus fulfilled these prophecies, and therefore only Christians could complete Judaism."[3] Matthew will argue that his own community's history marks the fulfilment of the prophecies of scripture: the new people are the true people; the "church" has replaced the "synagogue". In Matthew's account Jewish leaders are consistently presented in a negative light; his vigorous and sustained polemic against them is unrelieved throughout the narrative. This is a classic example of a breakaway group claiming legitimation for itself over the parent group. As Graham Stanton observes:

> Legitimation includes the use of polemic to denounce the parent group and to differentiate the new group . . . Legitimation includes the claim of the new group that it is *not* innovatory: it is the parent

---

[3] P. Fredriksen, *From Jesus to Christ* (New Haven: Yale University Press, 1990), 38.

group which has gone astray. The new group is the legitimate heir to shared traditions which are now reinterpreted in the light of new convictions.[4]

Following the claim to legitimation, Matthew's Jesus is much more concerned about the Law and its interpretation than in other Gospels. Jesus comes for the lost sheep of the House of Israel. In Matthew's Gospel the Sea of Galilee is a boundary between the Jews and the Gentiles; in Mark's Gospel the Sea of Galilee is seen not as a boundary but as a bridge which Jesus regularly crosses. In Matthew's text the outreach to non-Jews is played down: in the missionary discourse in chapter 10, the disciples' mission is articulated *by its limitation:* "Go nowhere among the Gentiles, and enter no town of the Samaritans, but go rather to the lost sheep of the house of Israel" (Matthew 10:5-6).

Matthew stands within an Israelite community: how can we be faithful to our own tradition and accept Jesus as Messiah? That confession of who Jesus is will move the community away from their Jewish roots into *ekklesia.* If Matthew is writing in Antioch, he must know the Pauline tradition. In the late second century, there are the Pseudo-Clementine writings, in which Paul is seen as the enemy and Peter the hero. Peter is portrayed as someone who had the right teaching and refused to eat with Gentiles; the narrative openly opposes Paul, accusing him of subverting the tradition by turning away from following of the Law, and opening the doors too readily and easily to Gentiles. Paul is portrayed as the anti-Christ. We know that Paul eventually leaves Antioch never to return, and he speaks of his controversy with Peter over the Gentiles when Peter comes to the city (Galatians 2:11-14).

If writing in Antioch, Matthew is facing similar problems in the same city. For a community rooted in Judaism, there is also a clear tension about how fast this community should open its doors to the crowds of new people, the Gentiles. The world of the early Jewish-Christians is changing fast – not so much because of their own pastoral outreach but because outsiders are crowding to join them. Some Christian groups insisted that the Gentiles who were going to be baptised should first be circumcised, while other groups insisted, following Paul's example, that this demand would be a denial of the Gospel. Given the importance Matthew ascribes to Jewish identity, would he have insisted on circumcision? David Sim argues that Gentiles would first have to be circumcised as a condition of being inducted into Matthew's community "in the same manner as those who were Jews by birth. Ethnicity was therefore part and parcel of

---

[4] G. Stanton, *A Gospel for a New People: Studies in Matthew* (Edinburgh: T&T Clark, 1992), 105.

Matthean Christianity and the Gospel which represented it."[5] While Matthew never discusses circumcision, his understanding of ethnic identity would have been more fluid and nuanced than Sim suggests. Given dramatic historical changes, Matthew's project is reworking the identity of those who are sons of Abraham into those who are defined as brothers and sisters of Jesus, subordinating ethnic differences to the idea of a new family of God in *ekklesia*. Whatever *ekklesia* is, it is not a new ethnic grouping. Further, as John Riches comments:

> The instruction of the Eleven in 28:18-20, a passage which includes some identification of entrance procedures into the community, refers explicitly to "teaching them to observe all that I have commanded you". The most reasonable inference is that it is Jesus' explicitly recorded and transmitted teaching which is normative for the community. On as contentious a matter as circumcision had become in the church after the Pauline mission, the absence of a specific command from Jesus (not least in a context where he does prescribe baptism, which is not in the Mosaic Law) would carry the presumption that it was not commanded.[6]

There is the new movement away from Israel to a community centred on Jesus – but is there a danger that the original Jewish-Christian community might lose the treasure they had? Will the original community end up being swamped by the new "invaders"? Will the new dominant voice and culture of the young Church, which is largely Gentile, lead the community away from its Jewish roots?

The story of the Canaanite woman in Matthew 15:21-28 summarises this challenge. Here Jesus, like the Christian leaders, is seen at first reluctant to minister to an unwelcome outsider, even though she expresses her faith in Jesus. Can we take in all these needy strange people from different cultural, ethnic backgrounds who are, like the Canaanite woman, invading our space? While the first instinct is to minister only to your own people, who share your race and spiritual roots, Matthew's answer, like that of Jesus, is finally yes. While affirming the continuity of the tradition (ministering to the lost sheep of the house of Israel) he also welcomes the new. Jesus *finally* welcomes the outsider and underlines what she brings to the encounter: "Great is your faith." This echoes Jesus' voice to another Gentile, the centurion: "Truly, I say to you, not even in Israel have I found such faith" (8:10).

---

[5] D. Sim, "Christianity and Ethnicity in the Gospel of Matthew", in M. Brett (ed.), *Ethnicity and the Bible* (Leiden: Brill, 1996), 195.

[6] J. Riches, *Conflicting Mythologies: Identity Formation in the Gospels of Mark and Matthew* (Edinburgh: T&T Clark, 1993), 220.

We have a Gospel in which there is no direct internal evidence of the identity of the author. In the list of twelve apostles Matthew is substituted for Levi: tradition has put together Matthew as tax collector (9:9) and the author of the Gospel, but historical criticism points out that there is a great deal of evidence that this Gospel was written by someone steeped in the Jewish writings, possibly a scribe. This Gospel is written in Greek by a highly intelligent Greek-speaking Jew who is totally at home in the Hebrew scriptures and can quote them at will. He uses Mark as one of his sources: of the 660 verses in Mark about 600 are used by Matthew. The time of writing is assigned to the penultimate decade of the first century: Peter and Paul are dead; the original witnesses of Jesus' ministry are probably all dead. This period is a time of great literary productivity: with the first witnesses dying, and the Gospel being preached in different languages and cultures, there is a clear urgency to set the tradition down in writing. The written word gradually takes over from the oral tradition; this is the time for consolidating the tradition.

Most modern scholars would see Matthew as a former scribe, totally at home in the Hebrew scriptures, now reinterpreting them for the new Christian mission, as well as welcoming the new insights brought by discipleship – exactly like the convert scribe the evangelist speaks about:

> Every scribe who has been trained for the kingdom is like a householder who brings out of his treasure what is new and what is old (Matthew 13:52).

In Table 3.1, which shows a selection of example texts, I have tried to offer a simple picture of Matthew's theological and pastoral commitment, which is to venerate the old, based on the Mosaic Law, and to welcome the new, based on the new things God is doing. What is new and surprising is not limited to the time of Matthew's writing; the evangelist sees the unexpected as a core part of the Jewish tradition he esteems, which is why he chooses the particular women he does for his genealogy. It is as if what is happening in Matthew's community has made him re-read the past, having an educated eye for how the past story was itself influenced and shaped by the unexpected. While the men provide a continuous Israelite descent, the women provide discontinuity in this line. God acts not only in continuity but in discontinuity, not only in the regular flow of events but in the unexpected and the new.

Table 3.1: **Matthew brings out of his treasure-house things old and new**

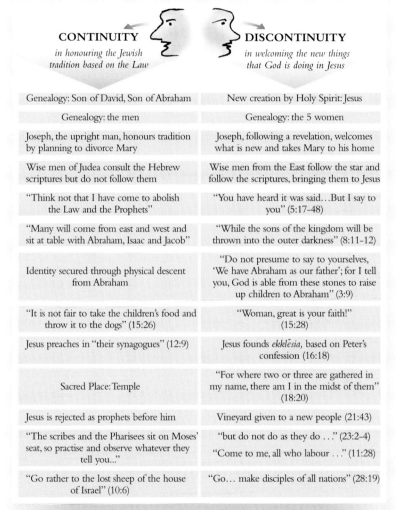

CONTINUITY in honouring the Jewish tradition based on the Law	DISCONTINUITY in welcoming the new things that God is doing in Jesus
Genealogy: Son of David, Son of Abraham	New creation by Holy Spirit: Jesus
Genealogy: the men	Genealogy: the 5 women
Joseph, the upright man, honours tradition by planning to divorce Mary	Joseph, following a revelation, welcomes what is new and takes Mary to his home
Wise men of Judea consult the Hebrew scriptures but do not follow them	Wise men from the East follow the star and follow the scriptures, bringing them to Jesus
"Think not that I have come to abolish the Law and the Prophets"	"You have heard it was said…But I say to you" (5:17-48)
"Many will come from east and west and sit at table with Abraham, Isaac and Jacob"	"While the sons of the kingdom will be thrown into the outer darkness" (8:11-12)
Identity secured through physical descent from Abraham	"Do not presume to say to yourselves, 'We have Abraham as our father'; for I tell you, God is able from these stones to raise up children to Abraham" (3:9)
"It is not fair to take the children's food and throw it to the dogs" (15:26)	"Woman, great is your faith!" (15:28)
Jesus preaches in "their synagogues" (12:9)	Jesus founds ekklēsia, based on Peter's confession (16:18)
Sacred Place: Temple	"For where two or three are gathered in my name, there am I in the midst of them" (18:20)
Jesus is rejected as prophets before him	Vineyard given to a new people (21:43)
"The scribes and the Pharisees sit on Moses' seat, so practise and observe whatever they tell you…"	"but do not do as they do …" (23:2-4) "Come to me, all who labour …" (11:28)
"Go rather to the lost sheep of the house of Israel" (10:6)	"Go… make disciples of all nations" (28:19)

The frame of Matthew: the Jewish story

Matthew begins his Gospel with the phrase *biblos geneseōs* – the book of the genesis or a record of the birth – immediately announcing the identity of Jesus as "son of David, the son of Abraham". He proceeds at a leisurely pace with Abraham, nineteenth-century BC, through a long list of names that serves as a link between the old story and the new, bringing him to his second frame of the infancy narrative. The genealogy is divided into three sections of fourteen generations: the patriarchs, from Abraham to David; the kings, from David to the Babylonian Exile; the unknown people, from the Babylonian Exile to Joseph. The triadic scheme of fourteen is obviously artificial: Matthew is probably employing the device of *gematria,* by which names are given numerical value. In Hebrew the name of David has three letters: ⁷ (daleth), ¹ (waw), and ⁷ (daleth), each of which is assigned a numerical (rather than a phonetic) value – in this case: 4, 6, and 4 respectively – the sum of which gives the numerical value to the name: 14. David's name is fourteenth on the list, and the fact that the name "David" appears before and after the genealogy suggests that David is the central key: the history of Israel culminates in the birth of the Messiah who is a descendant of the royal Davidic line.

The litany of names serves not only to anchor the identity of Jesus in the tradition of Israel but to see "Jesus who is called the Messiah" (Matthew 1:16) as the summit of that history. Thus for the Jewish members of Matthew's community, faith in Jesus did not mean the repudiation of their Jewish past but the acceptance of the new revelation that their past found its fulfilment in Jesus the Christ. Through the genealogy Jesus is characterised by his belonging to a particular bloodline, and that kinship forges his identity as part of a particular people. That lineage and kinship also, by adoption, become part of the story of all who are followers of the Christ.

The patriarchal figure of Abraham, however, provides ambiguity that serves Matthew's narrative well: although he is the great ancestor of a people who are defined by their belonging to a religious and ethnic group as well as belonging to the land, Abraham was born a Gentile who later abandoned his traditional religion, his kinship and his land, leaving all behind him, to forge a new identity as God's elected migrant. As John Riches observes, with a telling quote from Philo of Alexandria:

> Jews on the one hand have every reason to be proud of their ancestors, for they are shining lights to subsequent generations. On the other hand, Abraham's faithfulness to God is demonstrated

precisely by his willingness to abandon everything that binds him to his own people: "fellow-clansmen, or wardsmen, or schoolmates, or comrades, or blood relations on father's and mother's side, or country, or ancestral customs, or community of nurture or home life, all of them ties, possessing a power to allure and attract which is hard to throw off" (*De Abrahamo*, 67).[7]

While Matthew's presentation of Jesus as a son of Abraham establishes stability and continuity with the past, there is a subversive quality about the Abraham story which Jesus will follow with his disciples: they will leave home and kinship and land, to forge a new identity that is based, like Abraham, on doing the will of God. Although Abraham is a figure of stability as the patriarchal beginning for what is to come after him, he is also, paradoxically, a figure of subversion in the movement that he makes away from a secure and settled past. In order to become the person God wants him to be, he abandons the security of the past. Clearly he is a heroic figure for the Matthean Church.

In the first two chapters, Matthew obliges the reader with answering the basic questions of Jesus' identity, *Quis et unde?*[8] (Who are you and where are you from?) These two basic questions about a person's identity focus on kinship and land. Jesus' initial identity is announced by tabulating his descent from his Jewish ancestors, thus securing his belonging to a particular people (the first chapter); Matthew then shifts his focus to land showing Jesus belonging to a particular territory (the second chapter). The function of genealogy is not history but identity: it secures the Jewish identity of Jesus through kinship. While Abraham is celebrated as the great patriarch of the Jews, he is remembered as being more than this in the biblical narrative: before the covenant, before the Law, before Moses, Abraham is celebrated as the father of many nations. Matthew is securing him as the forefather of the new community of the Church.

---

[7] J. Riches, *Conflicting Mythologies*, 45.

[8] See the seminal article by K. Stendhal, "Quis et Unde? An Analysis of Matthew 1-2", in W. Eltester (ed.), *Judentum, Urchristentum, Kirche, Festschrift für J. Jeremias* (Berlin: Töpelmann, 1964), 94-105.

Table 3.2

THE FRAME OF MATTHEW'S GOSPEL

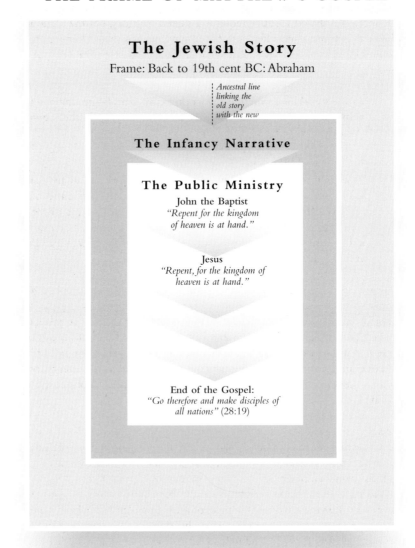

The Jewish Story
Frame: Back to 19th cent BC: Abraham

*Ancestral line
linking the
old story
with the new*

The Infancy Narrative

The Public Ministry
John the Baptist
*"Repent for the kingdom
of heaven is at hand."*

Jesus
*"Repent, for the kingdom of
heaven is at hand."*

End of the Gospel:
*"Go therefore and make disciples of
all nations"* (28:19)

Matthew's outer frame effectively constructs an identity for his own community. The Jews and Gentiles of Matthew's community do not, on the face of it, share either ancestral kinship or ancestral land: how do you construct a communal history so that both groups can claim a shared identity? If a shared identity requires a shared memory, Matthew adopts the past of Judaism and offers it to his community as a shared heritage: the genealogy will include Jew and Gentile. Dale Allison makes the point well:

> Matthew and his community, like other Christians before them, read themselves into the book and so came to make it their own. Matthew's Jesus, the son of David and the son of Abraham (1:1), by fulfilling the prophecies of the Jewish Bible and by being like Moses, became the heir of Jewish history and tradition (cf. 21:43), which in turn made his followers joint heirs of the same... Christians were uniting themselves to the sacred past of the Jews, the one people of God: to belong to Jesus Christ was to belong to Israel's history and so have their memories. In this way the Bible ceased to be the chronicle of a nation and became instead the charter of the church, a sort of legitimating aetiology.[9]

Matthew's genealogy, through the adoption of Judaism, roots his community in a distinguished past, validating the new enterprise of *ekklēsia* via antiquity. While the men provide a continuous Israelite descent in Matthew's genealogy, the women provide discontinuity in this line: *both* are part of the tradition. God acts not only in continuity but in discontinuity, not only in the regular flow of events but in the unexpected and the new, not only through Jews but through Gentiles. A brief look at the five women might prove instructive.

Tamar

A Canaanite woman, Tamar, marries Er, the first-born son of Judah (Genesis 38). Er commits some unidentified offence against God, and dies as a consequence of his action. Judah commands his second son, Onan, to do his duty and provide a child for his brother. While Onan is happy to sleep with Tamar, he has no intention of providing a child for his brother, so he practises *coitus interruptus*. What he does is regarded by God as offensive, and he dies for spilling his seed on the ground. Having lost two of his sons, Judah tells Tamar to return home as a widow and wait for his son Shelah to grow up; Judah, however, is determined not to lose his third son to this woman.

---

[9] D. Allison, *The New Moses: A Matthean Typology* (Edinburgh: T&T Clark, 1993), 278-279.

After a long time, Judah's wife dies, and some time later Judah travels to see the men he employs to shear his sheep. When Tamar hears this report she casts aside her widow's clothes, dresses as a prostitute, covering her face with a veil, and waits for Judah on the approach road to the town of Timnah, in the southern hills of Judah. Tamar realises that she will never see Shelah, so she sets a trap for her father-in-law, determined that she will not die childless. Judah takes her for a temple prostitute and asks to sleep with her: the only question is arithmetic. Judah promises a kid from his flock, and Tamar asks for a pledge until it is delivered to her, identifying three things: his seal, his belt and his stick.

When Tamar sleeps with Judah, she conceives by him; then returning home, she dresses again in her widow's weeds. Judah sends a friend with a kid to recover his pledge, but the village people assure him that they harbour no prostitute in the village. On hearing the news Judah agrees to let the unidentified woman keep his pledge; otherwise, he says, he will become a laughing-stock. Three months later, Judah is informed that his daughter-in-law has played the harlot and is now pregnant: he orders her to be burned alive. As Tamar is being led to her execution, she sends a message to her father-in-law: "It was the man to whom these things belong who made me pregnant. Look at them and see whose seal and belt and stick these are" (Genesis 38:25). Judah repents of his decision, admitting that Tamar is in the right. She gives birth to twins, Perez and Zerah, whom Matthew names among the ancestors of Jesus. By her initiative Tamar continues the line of Judah, and it is within this tribe that the kingship is entrusted to the house of David.

Rahab

If Tamar dressed up as a prostitute, Rahab is introduced as a professional one (Hebrew *zônâ*) in Joshua 2:1 (see also 6:17. 25). She is a Canaanite woman who lives detached from her clan. Joshua, the divinely designated successor to Moses, is planning to attack Jericho, his gateway to the Promised Land: he sends two spies into the city to gather intelligence. They stay at Rahab's house, which is built into the city wall, thus affording a discreet escape for her clients via a window, when needed, leaving them outside the city itself. The king of Jericho hears of their arrival and commands Rahab to give up her guest-spies, but she hides them in the roof, and answers the king that while the spies were indeed at her house, they disappeared before the city gate was closed at nightfall.

Rahab has heard of accounts of Israel's adventures in the desert and acknowledges to the spies the unique power of their God; it is because of this belief – not that she opposes the royal establishment in Jericho – that she has risked her life to save them. She extracts from the spies the promise that she, her family and household will be saved when the Israelites conquer the city. She is told to hang a scarlet cord from her window as a sign that her household is to be spared. She then lets the two spies down from a window with a rope, leaving them outside the city walls. At the time of the conquest, Joshua honours the agreement, and Rahab and her household, alone among the city's inhabitants, are spared. They are led to safety outside of the camp, and a final note records that "she dwelt in Israel to this day" (Joshua 6:25). This outsider facilitates Israel's entrance into the Promised Land.

By the end of the first century AD Rahab is celebrated in Christian literature for her faith (Hebrews 11:31) and for her good works (James 2:25).

Ruth
A family from Bethlehem – Elimelech, Naomi, and their two sons – journey to the land of Moab to escape the famine. The father dies, and the two sons take Moabite wives, Ruth and Orpah. After ten years, the two sons also die, leaving no offspring behind them. Bereft, Naomi decides to return to her native land because she has heard that God has visited her people and given them food. The three woman set out for the journey to Bethlehem.

On the way back, Naomi counsels her two daughters-in-law to return to their mothers' house with her blessing, insisting that she cannot provide husbands for them. Orpah returns, but Ruth decides to stay with Naomi:

> Where you go, I will go,
> and where you lodge, I will lodge;
> your people shall be my people,
> and your God, my God;
> where you die I will die
> and there will I be buried.
> May the Lord do so to me
> and more also,
> if even death parts me from you (Ruth 1:16-17).

They arrive in Bethlehem at the beginning of the barley harvest and Ruth immediately focuses on the task of finding food. Ruth gleans among the ears of corn in the field of a wealthy unmarried man named

Boaz, who belongs to the extended family of Elimelech. When Boaz hears who Ruth is, he assures her that he has ordered his servants not to molest her: in his fields she will be safe, and she should not glean in any other fields. He prays that her kindness to Naomi and her bravery will be rewarded by the God of Israel.

When Naomi hears the name of their new patron, she tells Ruth that Boaz is a relative and has the right of redemption over them. Naomi sees it as her duty to ensure that Ruth is happily settled in a new home, so later she tells Ruth to go to the threshing-floor, wait until Boaz eats and drinks, mark where he lies down, and then lift the blanket from his feet. When Boaz wakes in the middle of the night, Ruth identifies herself and says: "Spread your skirt of your cloak over your maidservant, for you are next of kin" (Ruth 3:9). Though willing, Boaz notes that there is another relative who has a prior right of redemption over Ruth: he tells Ruth to stay the night and in the morning her future will be determined. She lies at his feet.

The unnamed relative is agreeable to redeeming the land of Elimelech but not to purchasing Ruth the Moabitess, thus restoring Elimelech's name to his inheritance. Boaz takes the honour, and the elders give him their blessing saying: "May your house become like the house of Perez whom Tamar bore to Judah" (Ruth 4:12). Ruth bears a son to Boaz, whom they call Obed, and Naomi takes him to her bosom and becomes his nurse. Obed will continue the family line to become the grandfather of King David.

Uriah's wife

One evening King David takes a stroll on the palace roof, and when he is admiring the moonlit view his attention becomes focused on a particular scene, a remarkably beautiful woman bathing herself. When he enquires about the identity of the woman he is told that she is Bathsheba, the wife of Uriah the Hittite. Uriah is one of the warriors in King David's elite force of the "Thirty" (2 Samuel 23:24-39). David sends for Bathsheba, and when she attends him they end up sleeping together. She later sends David a message that she is with child.

David wants it to appear that Uriah is the father of Bathsheba's child, so he sends for his warrior and tells him to go to his house, rest, and food will be sent from the royal table. Uriah spends the night at the king's door, explaining to David that his commander Joab and his men are camping in the open fields, and he has no heart to benefit from comforts they do not enjoy. David makes him drunk, but Uriah stubbornly refuses to go home. The king gives Uriah a letter for Joab, who is ordered to place Uriah in the thick of battle and then withdraw his troops, leaving Uriah isolated. When Bathsheba hears of her husband's death she mourns her loss. With the period of mourning over, David sends for her and she becomes his wife. The child that she bore to David dies, but the second son of their union is Solomon, who will share with David the pinnacle of renown among the kings of Israel. What began as an adulterous liaison eventually results in the birth of the wisest king of Israel in Solomon, son of David.

Mary
"Jacob [was] the father of Joseph the husband of Mary, of whom Jesus was born, who is called Christ" (Matthew 1:16). Matthew's shift away from his genealogical formula (X was the father of Y) indicates that Joseph was not the biological father of Jesus; we must await an explanation for this unique exception, which is given in 1:18-25. In Genesis 10:1-32 "the descendants of" are listed immediately after the name of the man who is the progenitor; in Matthew's genealogy this formula holds true for everyone, even when the mother is mentioned (for example, "Judah was the father of Perez and Zerah, Tamar being their mother") with the notable exception of Jesus. The monotonous lilt is interrupted; with Jesus there is discontinuity. Mary's name appears before that of Jesus: she is the progenitor, with the specific claim "of whom Jesus was born".

In eight verses (1:18-25) Matthew asserts four times that Jesus is born without male participation. Joseph's negative reaction to the news that Mary is pregnant underlines the fact that he had no part in this conception. Like the previous four women, there are exceptional circumstances surrounding Mary in her relationships: Joseph himself will provide the reader with the demurring voice.

The first four women in Matthew's genealogy are regarded as foreigners: Tamar and Rahab are Canaanites, Ruth is a Moabite, and Bathsheba is not identified by her own name but as the wife of Uriah *the Hittite*; these four – rather than Sarah or Rebekah or Rachel – are probably elected by Matthew to celebrate the truth that Jesus, the Jewish Messiah, was related through his ancestry to the Gentiles. Mary, however, is not a foreigner, so the obvious question is: what do the *five* women have in common? All have something unconventional or irregular in their relationships with their partners, but in spite of that they succeed in continuing the line of the Messiah. All the women show initiative; they map out new paths to the future; they are more active than their male partners in complicated circumstances; they play an important role in furthering God's project, so that each is seen as a key player in God's providential plan. God's providence has a place for the unexpected and irregular, even for the scandalous and the immoral, all of which can be transformed by God's grace into blessing.

Further, as W. Weren points out:

> The stories about the five women all turn out well. Eventually, each woman is taken into her family again, or at the end of the story she obtains a position within society to which she did not belong before. Retrospectively, it becomes clear that the women were fully within their rights, and in their adventures a power is revealed that neither men nor women are themselves able to manifest: the power of the Most High, or the power of the Holy Spirit.[10]

As Matthew catalogues the names of Jesus' weird and wonderful ancestors in the genealogy, the reader notices that God's curious choices include cheats, prostitutes, thieves, adulterers and murderers. Behind every name there is a biography, and Matthew illustrates through biography that God's salvation comes through the foolish and the fragile, the crooked and the cracked. Anyone can play a part in God's plan, Jew and Gentile, "both bad and good" (Matthew 22:10), which makes for a chronicle that finds its fulfilment in Jesus, who is called the Christ.

The birth of Jesus Christ

Although Mary is accorded only one sentence in 1:18, she is key to understanding the unique identity of Jesus as the one who is conceived of the Holy Spirit: he is the one who has his origin in God. Joseph as "son of David" will provide Jesus' identity as a descendant of David, not through natural paternity but through legal paternity. Matthew opens the story noting that Mary is betrothed to Joseph, but before living together she is found to be with child by the Holy Spirit. As Raymond Brown comments:

> Matthew wants the reader to know more than do the characters in the story, so that the reader will not entertain for a moment the suspicion that grows in Joseph's mind... There is never a suggestion in Matthew or Luke that the Holy Spirit is the male element in a

---

[10] W. Weren, "The Five Women in Matthew's Genealogy", *Catholic Biblical Quarterly*, 59 (April 1997), 304.

union with Mary, supplying the husband's role of begetting. Not only is the Holy Spirit not male (feminine in Hebrew; neuter in Greek), but also the manner of begetting is implicitly creative rather than sexual.[11]

Clearly Joseph, whose life has been rudely interrupted by the news that his wife is pregnant and who has not yet been told what the reader has been told by Matthew, believes Mary to have committed adultery; hence his immediate resolve to divorce her – a decision that is introduced by noting that Joseph is a just man, who would want to observe the Law, particularly with regard to sexual relations (see Deuteronomy 22:13-27; 24:1). When Joseph decides to proceed with a divorce but not cause public shame to Mary by bringing public charges against her – in other words, not demand a trial to determine the cause of the pregnancy – his life is interrupted again, this time by an angel appearing in his dream. Matthew retains the focus on Joseph, not least perhaps because Joseph represents all those just Jews who, at the time of the Gospel's writing, are being asked to accept the new things God is doing in Jesus, who are being invited to go against their inclinations and uncritical obedience to the Law and see God's providence in events that, at first, seem irregular and extraordinary. That said, however, Matthew will argue that all this takes place to fulfil an ancient prophetic word.

Matthew interrupts his story of the annunciation to Joseph by noting that all this took place to fulfil the words spoken to the prophet: "Behold a virgin shall conceive and bear a son and shall call his name Immanuel" (Isaiah 7:14). Like the four other women in the genealogy, Mary is fulfilling God's will: against the Jewish accusation of the illegitimacy of Jesus, Matthew asserts that Mary's conception is not immoral but fulfils the word of God. Matthew chooses the Greek text, "the virgin" of Isaiah 7:14 over the Hebrew, "the young woman". Matthew's first fulfilment quotation (he will apply this usage twelve times to incidents in Jesus' life) underlines his belief that the identity of Jesus and the significance of his birth are best understood in the light of God's saving initiative. The names "Jesus" and "Immanuel" reveal the heart of Jesus' mission: he will save the people because he is "God with us". The promise of God's abiding presence at the beginning of the Jesus story will be the same promise that concludes the Jesus story: "And lo, I am with you always, to the close of the age" (Matthew 28:20).

Joseph is told by the angel to take Mary home as his wife, and when he wakes up, "he [does] as the angel of the Lord commanded him: he took

---

[11] R.E. Brown, *The Birth of the Messiah* (London: Chapman, 1993), 124.

his wife, but knew her not until she had borne a son; and he called his name Jesus" (1:25). Matthew does not specify the name of Joseph's hometown, noting in the next verse that Jesus was born in Bethlehem (2:1). Since Joseph takes Mary to his home where she gives birth to Jesus, it would appear in Matthew's narrative that Joseph's hometown is Bethlehem. In Matthew's account Jesus is born at home in Bethlehem; in Luke's account Joseph comes from Nazareth with Mary south to Bethlehem for the enrolment, where Jesus is born in a cave and laid in a manger (Luke 2:6-7). While Matthew has to move his story from Bethlehem to Nazareth, Luke has the opposite challenge in moving his story from Nazareth to Bethlehem. In both cases, however, Bethlehem is celebrated as the place of Jesus' birth: as the home of David and the place of his anointing, there is no more appropriate place for the birth of the one who has been introduced in Matthew's Gospel as "son of David" (Matthew 1:1).

The visit of the magi

Matthew passes over the actual birth of Jesus in silence: while the birth is anticipated in the annunciation to Joseph, it is mentioned as being already over in the story of the magi. Although Joseph enjoyed the focus of attention in the previous story, he is not even mentioned in this narrative; Mary's name is mentioned, but she plays a subsidiary role. The real focus is on two dramatically different responses to the birth of Jesus: one of acceptance, illustrated by the Gentiles – the magi who come from the east and worship the true king of the Jews; the other of rejection, shown by the Jewish authorities – King Herod, the chief priests and the scribes. This story will act like an overture not only to the main body of the Gospel but also to the experience of Matthew's Church, announcing the broad themes of Gentile acceptance and the Jewish authorities' rejection of Jesus. The first to pay homage to Jesus are Gentiles from the east, illustrating Jesus' later promise: "Many will come from east and west and sit at table with Abraham, Isaac, and Jacob in the kingdom of heaven" (8:11).

The country of origin of the mysterious magi is not specified – traditional guesses focus on three places: Arabia (the gifts of gold and frankincense, mentioned by Isaiah 60:6, are associated with camel trains travelling from Arabia, and among the kings who offer royal gifts and the nations who do homage in Psalm 72, the gold or frankincense that is specified comes from Sheba, in south-west Arabia); Babylon (after the return from Exile a colony of Jews remained behind, so that their messianic expectations may have become known to local astrologers); Persia (the name *magoi* was originally associated with the Medes and Persians[12]). Neither is their number given, popularly presumed to be three from the count of their gifts, although eastern tradition numbers them as twelve. Their function, however, is clear in Matthew's narrative: they represent the spiritual elite of the Gentile world, the ancestors of all foreigners who will find their true destination in Jesus. If Abraham was the "father of a multitude of nations" (Genesis 17:5), this "son of Abraham" (Matthew 1:1) is seen at his birth as the one in whom all nations are blessed.

The magi, in their turn, have an ancestor in another non-Israelite magus "from the east" – Balaam, who is called by King Balak to pronounce a curse against the Israelites, "since they are too mighty for me" (Numbers 22:6). After an initial refusal, Balaam sets out with two servants: three men from the east travel with the chiefs sent by the king. On arrival Balaam refuses to become the ally of the king by cursing the Israelites; instead, he follows the divine revelation he has been given and blesses the enemies of the king, prophesying the nation's future greatness and the coming of a great ruler:

> Water shall flow from his buckets,
> and his seed shall be in many waters,
> his king shall be higher than Agag,
> and his kingdom shall be exalted.
> God brings him out of Egypt . . .
>
> I see him, but not now;
> I behold him, but not nigh:
> a star shall come forth out of Jacob,
> and a sceptre shall rise out of Israel (Numbers 24:7-8. 17).

Not daring to harm such a powerful seer, the disappointed king returns to his palace, while Balaam leaves and returns home. Balaam's prophecy probably refers to the emergence of the Davidic monarchy: King David is the star and the sceptre that rules over a united kingdom. In later Judaism, especially in the targums, Balaam's prophecy was interpreted as a reference to the Messiah, the anointed Davidic king. In Matthew's narrative the magi see the star's rising, signalling the birth of the infant king of the Jews; this is immediately interpreted as the birth of the Davidic Messiah (2:2). Herod, the reigning king, will attempt to destroy the new Davidic king by employing the help of foreign magi, but they refuse to collude with him and, like Balaam before them, honour the king's rival and then return home.

---

[12] When Emperor Justinian rebuilt the church at Bethlehem, the outline of the present Basilica, the façade was redecorated with images of the magi. When the Persians in 614 attacked the Holy Land, they did not destroy the Basilica at Bethlehem when they saw the magi depicted in the familiar dress of their own people.

It was a common motif in the ancient world that a new star marked the birth of a ruler: the astrological sign in Matthew's narrative, a sign of nature, moves the magi, as it did Balaam before them, to see the significance of the Davidic star. Their instinct is not to sit and discuss this new phenomenon but to follow it, to welcome this new heavenly sign as their teacher. The star, however, does not *by itself* lead the Gentile seekers to the place of the birth: the Gentiles must first go to the Jews and learn from them, through a revelation in the scriptures, the truth of God's providential plan. It will be through a combination of sources – a sign from nature and God's revelation contained in the Jewish scriptures – that the magi will reach their destination in Jesus.

So it is in Matthew's narrative that the star does not lead the magi directly to Bethlehem, but instead their journey leads them five miles north to the city of Jerusalem, where they seem to enjoy ready access to King Herod and his court. Herod the Great reigned from 37 to 4 BC, and, through his political acumen and consummate diplomacy with the Romans, managed to be granted the title "king of the Jews" – one he jealously guarded to the extent of murdering three of his sons. The magi are not seen to pay homage to King Herod or offer him gifts, in dramatic contrast to their later act of prostrating themselves in worship before the infant king of the Jews and presenting him with royal gifts. Instead, the magi pragmatically move to business at hand and make no secret of why they have come, to offer homage to the infant king of the Jews. On hearing the news the establishment of Judea gathers in an aristocratic huddle of discontent. The outsiders have unsettled the institution: the scene is set for conflict.

It may not appear to be a particularly wise move to tell the reigning king of the Jews that you are looking for the new one! On hearing the news, Herod is perturbed – a predictable reaction in the circumstances, given that his throne seems to be in immediate danger – and his anxiety is shared by the whole city of Jerusalem. Matthew appears to illustrate, as he will do later in his passion narrative, official Judaism united in their opposition to Jesus.

In response to the startling revelation Herod calls together the wise men of Judea – the chief priests and the scribes – to discover the birthplace of the Messiah. In uncovering the secret from the scriptures, the future enemies of Jesus now ironically testify to the birth of Jesus and his messiahship: the shepherd of Israel is to be born in Bethlehem, the city from which another shepherd, King David, came and where he was anointed. Matthew sounds notes and introduces themes here in his overture to the Gospel that will be developed later in the story. In the passion narrative it is foretold that Jesus the shepherd will be struck down and his sheep scattered (Matthew 26:31). More dramatically, the chief priests and the scribes and the elders will stand united before the crucified Jesus – above whose head is the charge, "This is Jesus, the King of the Jews" – and they will mock him, "He is the king of Israel" (Matthew 27:42). It will be a Gentile centurion, following the death of Jesus and another sign from nature in an earthquake, who will identify Jesus as a son of God (27:54).

Herod now summons the wise men and sees them secretly, to learn the exact date on which the star appeared; here Matthew prepares for the Herod's command to kill all male children two years old and under, "according to the time which he had ascertained from the wise men" (2:16). Having discovered the secret from the Jewish wise men about the place of the birth, and having discovered the secret from the Gentile wise men of the time of the star's rising, Herod now commands the magi to find out everything about the child, return and report all to him, so that he can offer this child king due homage. Herod's assumption that these foreign magi would become his informants and accomplices seems out of character for such a cunning king: it does not seem beyond the wit of Herod to send spies to follow the magi the five miles to Bethlehem; otherwise, it would hardly be difficult to identify the address of a house in a small Judean village, one which is marked by the arrival of a caravan of magi, carrying treasures from the east, and identified by a star!

As the magi set out south for Bethlehem, to their delight the star appears again as their guide and halts over the place where the child is. Why did the star not lead them here in the first place, without a detour to Jerusalem, thus avoiding the massacre of the innocents? A star halting over a particular address seems unusual, and trying to uncover astronomical phenomena at the time to explain this – such as the conjunction of Jupiter and Saturn in 7 BC – seems a diversion from Matthew's theological motif.[13] Matthew's star seems less of a celestial phenomenon when it identifies a particular house: if the ancients regarded stars as animate beings, and Jews tended to identify them with angels (Job 38:7), this star functions more like the angelic guide of the Exodus, whose function is to bring the expedition "to the place which I have prepared" (Exodus 23:20).

---

[13] See R. Brown's excursus on the possible explanations, *The Birth of the Messiah*, 170-173; 610-613.

The magi enter the marked house, and on seeing the child with his mother Mary, they wordlessly fall on their knees and do him homage. This child is their real destination, their determined focus, the object of their worship. They open their treasures now and offer their exotic gifts to *this* king. Whatever their plans were, a dream instructs them not to return to Herod and so become his accomplices: thus they return to their own country by a different way (Matthew 2:12).

Matthew develops the scene with the care of a master storyteller. He ranges the wise men who follow natural means – a star – against the wise men of Judea who are able to follow their own sign – the scriptures. It is clear from the story that the wise men of Judea have enough information in the scriptures to discover the place where the new Davidic king will be born; but their discovery is useless, for it does not lead them to homage. They are not disposed to act on what has been revealed. By contrast, the pagan strangers, after they have gone as far as they can in following the star, are willing to be instructed in a scripture that is foreign to them. They act on what has been given to them, and their journey leads them to their destination.

Matthew shows how two wisdoms collide: the wisdom of the Jewish institution and the wisdom of the pagan strangers. The wise strangers pass by the institution: their destination is not the exotic palace of the king but a child; their journey's end is not the institution of power but the person of Jesus.

For Matthew, the wise strangers are the vanguard of all peoples who make their own journey to God in Christ. They may have taken a route that seemed curious to a religious establishment that had so many antique maps in their possession; but God draws all sorts of different people to him by all sorts of different routes. The wandering magi were led to God more by natural wonder than dogmatic instruction, and this has made them symbols of hope for all who struggle to God by strange routes. A prayer to the magi, which Evelyn Waugh wrote for St Helena, catches something of this hope:

> You are my especial patrons... and patrons of all latecomers, of all who have a tedious journey to make to the truth, of all who are confused with knowledge and speculation, of all who through politeness make themselves partners in guilt, of all who stand in danger by reason of their talents...
> For his sake who did not reject your curious gifts, pray always for all

the learned, the oblique, the delicate. Let them not be quite forgotten at the Throne of God when the simple come into their kingdom.[14]

The flight into Egypt

From the exotic scene of gift-giving we move to a desperate scene of murder and flight. The family's escape is prompted by the appearance of an angel in Joseph's dream, warning him of Herod's intentions to kill the child, and commanding Joseph to flee to Egypt and stay there until he is alerted it is safe to return. Herod's power had no sway in Egypt, which had been under direct Roman control since 30 BC, and although the dominant memory of Egypt for the Israelites was as a place of bondage, it also served as a popular place of refuge – for instance, when Solomon heard that Jeroboam was plotting against him, the king condemned him to death, and Jeroboam "fled to Egypt" (1 Kings 11:40), where the Pharaoh granted him political asylum.

In escaping to Egypt, Joseph is again seen to follow his dream, carrying out the angel's command. One of the characteristic elements in the story of the patriarchs is the frequent use of dreams in which they are called upon to face hardship and adversity that will challenge their capacity and commitment: four times Joseph is diverted, through his dreams, to take other roads (Matthew 1:20; 2:13. 19. 22). He would remind Matthew's readers of Joseph in the Old Testament, "this dreamer" (Genesis 37:19) who went to Egypt to escape with his life and later saved his family by bringing them to Egypt: again the image of Egypt as refuge. Jesus is seen symbolically to relive the Old Testament story not only of Joseph going to Egypt but also of Israel returning from there in the Exodus.

Matthew adds the editorial comment that this happened to fulfil what the Lord had spoken to the prophet: "Out of Egypt have I called my son" (Matthew 2:15; see Hosea 11:1, "When Israel was a child, I loved him, and out of Egypt I called my son"). The quotation originally referred to God's calling Israel, his son, from Egypt at the time of the Exodus. Matthew clearly sees Jesus recapitulating the experience of Israel: Jesus is the embodiment of the true Israel. Meier comments on the significance of the quotation from Hosea:

> This citation is the theological highpoint of the infancy narrative, because here Jesus receives his most exalted definition. While certainly son of David, son of Abraham, son of Mary, son of Joseph,

---

[14] E. Waugh, *Helena* (London: Chapman & Hall, 1950), 239.

Jesus the true Israel is above all "my son" i.e., Son of God. Like Israel, God's Son, Jesus the true Son undergoes an Exodus from Egypt, passes through the waters of the Jordan, and is tempted in the desert.[15]

While Matthew's reading of Hosea goes beyond the original meaning of the text, it serves his theme of continuity well, connecting the new Jesus story to the ancient story of Israel. This is developed further in his use of the story of Moses. As Joseph was the one who brought his people into Egypt, Moses is the reason why they leave. By the first century AD the story of Moses had been developed: we know this through the writing of Philo and Josephus. In the expanded narrative Pharaoh was warned by astrologers/wise men that a liberator of Israel was about to be born who would threaten his crown. Pharaoh and his advisers decided that the best way to safeguard the throne was to kill all the Hebrew male children. At the same time Moses' father receives notice in a dream that his pregnant wife will bear the child who will save Israel. Forewarned, the parents save the life of their child. Jesus, like Moses before him, begins his life as a refugee in flight from a wicked king. In Table 3.3 I have listed the main points of contact between the two stories – a more comprehensive list is supplied by Dale Allison in his study of Matthean typology[16] that includes the possibility of a tradition about the virgin birth of Moses.

Outwitted by the wise men, King Herod orders the slaughter of all male children who are two years or younger. Although the massacre of the children is in keeping with Herod's character – he did not hesitate to execute anyone who threatened his throne – there is no independent witness to Matthew's story in extant literature; Josephus, who catalogues the horrors of Herod's reign, makes no mention of it. As the massacre of the children refers back to the persecution of the Israelites in Egypt, so the reference to Rachel and Ramah refers back to the story of the Exile. Following the destruction of Jerusalem in 586 BC, Ramah served as a staging-post for some Jewish groups on their way to deportation in Babylon (Jeremiah 40:1). At Ramah the prophet Jeremiah witnessed the departure of his comrades, inspiring his oracle quoted by Matthew, which associates the lamentations of the exiles with those of Rachel, whose tomb was nearby (see 1 Samuel 10:2). Although Ramah is to the north of Jerusalem and Bethlehem is to the south, Matthew associates Rachel with Bethlehem, an association that can be seen today in the Muslim shrine of Rachel's tomb, on the approach road to Bethlehem.

---

[15] J.P. Meier, *Matthew* (Dublin: Veritas, 1980), 14.

[16] See D. Allison, *The New Moses*, 142-146.

Table 3.3

MOSES	JESUS
In the expanded tradition mentioned by Josephus in *Antiquities* 2.210-16, Amran, the pious father of Moses, is worried about his wife's pregnancy after hearing that Pharaoh has ordered the death of Hebrew male infants. God appears to him in a dream, counsels him not to despair, and prophesies his son's future greatness.	Joseph, the just father of Jesus, is concerned about his wife's pregnancy and is planning to divorce her. The angel of the Lord appears to him in a dream, counsels him not to be afraid, and prophesies his son's future greatness.
Moses is celebrated as the great "saviour" of the people of Israel.	"You shall call his name Jesus, for he will save his people from their sins" (Matthew 1:21).
In *Antiquities* 2.205, 234, Josephus says that Pharaoh heard of Israel's new liberator from learned scribes. In the Jerusalem targum on Exodus 1:15, the two magicians, who are sons of Balaam, are the source of the information.	King Herod hears of the birth of the King of the Jews from the chief priests, the scribes, and the magi.
When Pharaoh hears the prophecy of the liberator, he is "seized with fear" (*Antiquities* 2.206).	"When King Herod heard this he was troubled, and all Jerusalem with him" (Matthew 2:3).
At the time of the birth of Moses, Pharaoh gives the order to slaughter every male Hebrew child (Exodus 1).	Around the time of Jesus' birth, Herod orders the slaughter of all male children two years and under (Matthew 2:16).
Moses is kept safe as an infant by divine providence. Later he must flee his homeland because Pharaoh seeks to kill him (Exodus 2:1-10).	By divine providence Jesus is kept safe and is taken from his homeland because Herod seeks to kill him (Matthew 2:13-14).
Following the death of Pharaoh, Moses is commanded by God to return to Egypt, "for all those who wanted to kill you are dead" (Exodus 4:19).	Following the death of Herod, Joseph is commanded by an angel to return to Israel, "for those who sought the child's life are dead" (Matthew 2:19-20).
Moses takes his wife and child and returns from exile to Egypt (Exodus 4:20).	Joseph takes his wife and son and returns from exile to Israel (Matthew 2:21).

The three places that are mentioned in Matthew's scriptural quotations – *Bethlehem,* the city of David, *Egypt,* the land of the Exodus, and *Ramah,* the mourning staging-post of the Exile – present a geographical microcosm of the history of Israel. That history is now recapitulated in the story of Jesus, one that is celebrated as being not only in theological continuity with the story of Israel but its fulfilment.

Finally, by way of comment on this passage, it may be worth noting an incident that is said to have taken place before the birth in 63 BC of Gaius Octavian, who later became the Emperor Augustus, and was celebrated in the Roman imperial cult[17] as a son of God and the saviour of mankind:

> A few months before Augustus was born a portent was generally observed in Rome, which gave warning that nature was pregnant with a king for the Roman people. Thereupon the senate in consternation decreed that no male child born that year should be reared. But those whose wives were with child ensured that the decree was not filed in the treasury, since each one appropriated the prediction to his own family.[18]

This account has interesting parallels with Matthew's story of the Herodian plot: a portent announces the birth of a new king; officialdom is thrown into confusion; a decree is made for the execution of all newly born male children, to safeguard the current regime; the person to whom the decree was specifically aimed was spared. Later, Augustus is credited as saying of King Herod that it was better to be his pig (*hus* in Greek) than his son (*huios*) – anecdotal testimony to how widespread the knowledge had circulated about Herod's unrelieved brutality.[19]

From Egypt to Nazareth

Following the death of Herod the Great, Joseph is again instructed through a dream to take a new road: "Rise, take the child and his mother, and go to the land of Israel, for those who sought the child's life are dead" (Matthew 2:20; see Exodus 4:19). Without demur, Joseph acts promptly: again Joseph is presented as the obedient Jew who follows this new word of the Lord as he heads back for Israel. Joseph naturally starts to head for Judea, presumably to Bethlehem where he has his home, but when he hears – we are not told the source – that Archelaus now rules over the region of Judea, he is afraid to go there.

---

[17] See my note on the Priene inscription in previous chapter.

[18] Suetonius, *Lives,* Augustus 2.94.3.

[19] Attributed to the Latin writer, Macrobius (c. AD 400) *Saturnalia* 2.4.2. "When [Augustus] heard that Herod king of the Jews had ordered all the boys in Syria under the age of two years to be put to death and that the king's son was among those killed, he said, 'I'd rather be Herod's pig than Herod's son'."

King Herod died in 4 BC – it seems a puzzle, particularly considering Matthew's account, that Herod's death should be before the time of Christ! The system of dating events before and after the birth of Christ was constructed by a monk, Dionysius Exiguus (Denis the Small), at the beginning of the sixth century. Sadly, his arithmetic proved somewhat faulty. He calculated that the birth of Christ was 753 AUC (*ab urbe condita*), that is, 753 years from the foundation of the city of Rome. In fact, Herod died four years before that, in 749 AUC, hence the calculation that he died in 4 BC. The year Herod died is the latest date for the calculation of Jesus' birth; it may well have been as early as 9 BC.

In the final version of his will Herod named Archelaus as principal heir to his kingdom.[20] Archelaus refrained from using the royal title "king" – one that could be bestowed only by the emperor Augustus – but was soon faced with demands for the reduction and abolition of taxes, the release of prisoners, and the replacement of the high priest appointed by his father. In order to settle the serious unrest that followed, Archelaus ordered his cavalry into the Temple precincts: they killed 3,000 Jews in a bloodthirsty purge.[21]

Archelaus sailed to Rome to petition Augustus for his father's throne. During his absence, the civil unrest developed into widespread rebellion. The Roman governor of Syria, Varus, restored order and also gave permission for a Jewish delegation to sail to Rome to oppose the claim of Archelaus: they requested that Judea be annexed and ruled directly from Rome.[22] Augustus compromised: he divided Herod's property, probably to ensure the future of Herod's dependants and go some way to satisfy the Jewish delegation that demanded abolition of the monarchy. He awarded the title of *ethnarch* (leader of a race) to Archelaus, with the territories of Judea, Samaria and Idumea, together with a number of cities, including Jerusalem. Antipas was confirmed as *tetrarch* (leader of a quarter) of the regions Galilee and Perea; Philip as *tetrarch* of the areas north and west of the Sea of Galilee.

Although Archelaus did not gain the title king, it is interesting to note that Josephus calls him "king" – which might be a popular indication of the scope of Archelaus' power. On his return he exacted a cruel revenge on his opponents. Speaking of Archelaus' tyrannical rule, Josephus notes how Archelaus, "remembering past differences, behaved savagely not only towards Jews but also towards the Samaritans".[23] He remained in office only ten years, until AD 6. Because of Archelaus' stubborn commitment to violence as his principal form of government, Augustus summoned the

[20] Josephus, *Antiquities* 17.188-189.
[21] Josephus, *Antiquities* 17.218.
[22] Josephus, *Antiquities* 17.299-314.
[23] Josephus, *Jewish War* 2.111.

ethnarch to Rome, exiled him to Vienne in Gaul, and appointed a Roman procurator to govern his territories. It might be worth noting, however, that the tomb of Archelaus was later pointed out to visitors at Bethlehem![24]

Another dream intervenes to divert Joseph from his chosen path, this time instructing him to go to Galilee, a region traditionally known as Galilee of the Gentiles (see Matthew 4:15, quoting Isaiah 8:23 – 9:1). Ruled by Herod Antipas, a full brother of Archelaus, from 4 BC until AD 39, Galilee enjoyed a more peaceful political climate than Judea. As Sean Freyne notes:

> One highly significant aspect of Antipas' reign is the fact that its stability meant that there was no need for direct Roman intervention in the internal life of the province. In view of the military, financial and social upheavals of the previous period this was indeed a great blessing for the ordinary people, and stands in sharp contrast to the situation in Judea, where the insensitivity and brutality of the Roman procurators make a sorry story of mismanagement, and is generally accepted as one of the major immediate causes for the revolt in 66 C.E.[25]

Joseph withdraws (*anachōrein*) to the region of Galilee. Matthew tends to use this verb when Jesus leaves a place because of people's unbelief (see 2:14; 4:12; 12:15; 14:13; 15:21): it will be used in later Christianity as a technical term for monasticism (anchorites) as a withdrawal from public life into contemplation. Joseph settles in a town called Nazareth in fulfilment of the prophetic word: "He will be called a Nazarene" (Matthew 2:23). Although scholars can find no equivalent line in any passage of the Old Testament,[26] Matthew concludes his infancy narrative with the name that will for ever identify the son of David, the son of Abraham, the Son of God: Jesus of Nazareth. Matthew closes his infancy narrative having effectively moved the family from exile back to *Israel,* north to *Galilee,* and specifically to the town of *Nazareth.* That geographical map puts Jesus in place for the beginning of his public ministry.

Conclusion

In these first two chapters that make up the beginning of Matthew's Gospel, the evangelist has set the scene with the care of an accomplished dramatist for the emergence of Jesus in his public ministry. When Jesus appears on the public stage as an adult, we will not be asking the questions

---

[24] Josephus, *Antiquities* 17.342-44.

[25] S. Freyne, *Galilee from Alexander the Great to Hadrian* (Edinburgh: T&T Clark, 1998), 68.

[26] Isaiah 11:1 has been suggested: "There shall come forth a shoot from the stump of Jesse, and a branch (*nēser*) shall grow out of his roots." The branch is identified as the child Immanuel, whose approaching birth is announced in Isaiah 7:14, which Matthew has already quoted in 1:23.

that disturb so many of the participants in the story: "Who is this man? Where does he come from?" We the readers have been well informed about his identity and background from our theologian and guide, Matthew. As in Mark's preface, we are the privileged insiders to the insights the evangelist shares with us, insights that are not available to participants in the ensuing drama.

In Matthew's tapestry of stories, we see how the Old Testament meets the New, not as rivals but as theological associates; we understand how the story of Israel is connected through the genealogy from its beginning with the patriarch Abraham to Jesus, son of Abraham, while at the same time observing the presence of Gentile women in that lineage; we notice how, after the patrilineal genealogy is established, the messiah is born of a virgin; we see how the beginning of the Moses story and the Exodus are superimposed on the beginning of the Jesus story, so that Jesus recapitulates key moments in Israel's history; we hear the ancient prophetic voices that are cited as testimony to the truth that what is happening is in fulfilment of God's providential plan.

In all this we learn that the new events taking place are not altogether new but the legitimate heir to shared traditions from the beginning of Israel. For Matthew the past is not a burden to be liberated from; rather, he appropriates it, using it as a life-giving source and legitimation of his own community. He illustrates the teaching he esteems: "Every scribe who has been trained for the kingdom of heaven is like a householder who brings out of his treasure what is new and what is old" (Matthew 13:52). Although there is discontinuity – Matthew has lived long enough in the Church to know that history has moved on – paradoxically, he stubbornly maintains his expansive insight that even the discontinuity has resonance with the past. Matthew's newness is not novelty, but the newness of completion: thus, no matter how combative his tone in the knowledge that the Jewish rejection of the Gospel is pervasive, he never dissociates the new Jesus movement from its roots in Judaism.

Even while official Judaism is seen to reject Jesus in the infancy narrative – the new family group is distanced into exile from its parent religious group, ending up as refugees – Matthew's presentation of Joseph, a descendant of Abraham and David, to the reader is written in sharp contrast to that of officialdom. As the upright Jewish character who scrupulously observes the Law – the key figure in connecting the whole infancy narrative – Joseph's life is interrupted five times, four of which are in the form of dreams; but he always responds with immediate obedience to the new direction, ending up eventually, clearly not his chosen destination, in Galilee of the Gentiles. He never stays stubbornly fixed to his own way: he is the patron saint of all who have to adjust their lives to new circumstances, of all who have to leave home and change direction to safeguard the lives of their loved ones.

Joseph acts as a representative for all upright Jews in Matthew's community who have welcomed and followed what is newly revealed in the story of Jesus, even if that diverts them from beliefs and plans they previously cherished, and even if they end up as exiles from their parent religious group, in a growing Gentile community. Following the rupture with the new Pharisaic Judaism, Matthew's community, a new minority grouping, will have to differentiate and distance themselves from their larger parent group while, at the same time, honouring the sacred tradition both groups share. I find it worth noting that the evangelist will end his Gospel narrative with another brave Joseph, an upright Jewish figure who has become a disciple of Jesus, one who stands apart from the destructive campaign of Jewish officialdom and goes to the Roman governor for permission to bury the body of Jesus, wraps it in a clean shroud, and places it in his own new tomb (Matthew 27:57-60). As Jesus' birth is safeguarded by one Joseph, so his burial is secured by another.

At the same time, the magi in the infancy narrative will figure as representative of all foreigners in Matthew's community who have found, after diverse routes, their eventual destination in Jesus and who come to join a small Jewish group already there. These unidentified magi are the exotic forerunners of the universal Church. In that sense Matthew's dramatisation of the birth of Jesus connects exquisitely with the drama in his own struggling community to find its own identity: there is continuity and discontinuity, rupture and fulfilment, belonging and exile, faith and apprehension, celebration and lamentation. It is not a narrative without struggle or conflict; neither is it a story without beauty or harmony. Emerging from the mix and apparent muddle of these diverse events and people, there is Gospel.

The notes that Matthew sounds in this overture to his Gospel – including vaguely familiar phrases that are reprised from ancient scores, discordant passages that warn of sorrowful things to come, all overwhelmed by an original score – really do prove to be a majestic and moving proclamation of the main composition of his work. Just as the ultimate power of King Herod, solemnly decreeing the death of the infant King of the Jews, does not have the final say about the future of Jesus, neither will the ultimate power of the Roman governor, solemnly declaring the death of the King of the Jews, have the last word about Jesus of Nazareth. And, finally, just as the first visitors to Jesus are foreigners from far beyond the hills of Judea, so Matthew's church will grow in the risen Lord's command to make disciples of all nations and in the assurance of his promise: "I am with you always, to the close of the age" (Matthew 28:20).

4 The beginning of Luke

Introduction

On the hot summer night of 18 July in the year AD 64 a fire broke out in the arcade of shops surrounding the Circus Maximus, Rome's chariot stadium. Within minutes, the tinder-dry stadium was ablaze, and the fire spread quickly through the densely populated *insulae* of the city: most Romans lived in houses constructed of wood that were set along the narrow streets and alleyways of the city. With over a million inhabitants living in the city, many in densely populated slum quarters, several thousand perished in the flames, were smothered by smoke, or were buried beneath the charred ruins. The flames raged for six days before they came under control; then the fire reignited and burned for another three days. After the desolation, two-thirds of the imperial city lay in ruins: ten of Rome's fourteen districts lay wasted.[1]

Rumour spread like the fire itself that the mad emperor, Nero, was to blame: it was well known that Nero wanted to bypass the senate and rebuild the squalid centre of the city to his own liking, something he achieved in the wake of the fire when he built the Domus Aurea, a majestic series of palatial villas and pavilions set in a landscaped park. When the fire began, the emperor was miles away, in his villa at the cooler coastal resort at Anzio: it is Tacitus, the aristocratic historian and anti-imperialist, who kept alive the rumour that Nero watched Rome burn while he composed an ode to the flaming city, playing on his lyre, although the historian claims that the rumour that Nero ordered the fire was unsubstantiated and based on the population's deep distrust of the emperor.

Well aware of his growing unpopularity among the people and the rumours spread by the surviving homeless that he was an imperial arsonist, Nero sought to divert suspicion away from himself, so he looked for victims to blame. His choice fell on a new Jewish sect called the Christians: earlier, in AD 49, the Emperor Claudius had banished a number of them from Rome because they were causing angry disputes in the Jewish synagogues of the city with their arguments about the Christ. The fact that some people in this sect were teaching that the Christ would come soon and that the end of the world would happen by fire seemed a useful basis on which to believe that the members of this sect started the fire to realise the prophecy. The incendiarists were arrested and thrown into prison, to await their fate.

---

[1] Accounts of the fire can be found in Tacitus, *Annals* 15:38ff; Suetonius, *Life of Nero* (chapter 38); Dio Cassius, *Roman History* (chapter 62).

Thus began the first great persecution of Christians. Nero slaughtered Christians by the hundreds: fastened to crosses, they were set on fire to illuminate a circus which Nero staged in his own gardens; others were covered with the skins of wild beasts and torn to death by dogs for the crowd's amusement; some were crucified on the roads leading into the city; yet others were thrown into gladiatorial combat or to the lions. The two principal apostles of the emerging Church, Peter and Paul, were martyred in this persecution. Yet, paradoxically, when news of the persecution spread though the empire, many people heard for the first time of the name of Jesus: not for the first time, persecution proved a potent advertisement for the new religion.

For the second time in Rome, the governing power learned to distinguish Christianity from Judaism. Before the fire, Christianity was tolerated as a sect of Judaism; after the fire, the Christians suddenly became the minority to blame for everything. The majority of Christians were not punished for the crime of incendiarism, but were put to death, according to Tacitus, for their anti-social tendencies: they were regarded as enemies of the social order, whose practices were said to endanger civilised society.[2]

Once Nero's persecution ended, Christianity was still recognised as an illegal religion. While the Church was adapting to its illegal status within the Roman Empire, the first great defence of Christianity was written – the two-volume work of the Gospel of Luke and the Acts of the Apostles. Both writings are dedicated to an unknown high Roman official, his excellency Theophilus; they are the first Christian writings dedicated to the world outside Christianity. They defend Christianity against the accusations of the Romans.

Luke's Gospel will tell how Christ turned his back on political revolution to accomplish a more profound revolution in the heart of people. Are Christians suspected of anti-social behaviour? Luke will portray the founder of Christianity as a figure of nobility, grace and charm; a man who breathed kindliness and graciousness. Luke will show that Jesus and his followers were found innocent by the representatives of the Roman law: Pilate declares three times that Jesus is innocent of the charges brought against him (Luke 23:4. 14. 15). Whereas Mark's Roman centurion at the crucifixion declares that Jesus is truly God's son (Mark 15:39), Luke's Roman centurion declares: "Certainly this man was innocent!" (Luke 23:47). In the Acts of the Apostles Roman officials are repeatedly represented as finding no serious fault with the Christian

---

[2] See Tacitus, *Annals* 15.44.

movement: for example, when Paul is taken captive, Felix, the procurator of Judea, responds kindly to him (Acts 24:22-23); Festus, who succeeds Felix, grants Paul's appeal to Caesar (Acts 25:12) and defends Paul, before King Agrippa, arguing: "I found that he had done nothing deserving death" (25:25); when the whole trial council retires to confer, they agree: "This man is doing nothing to deserve death or imprisonment" (Acts 26:31). In Luke's apologetic perspective, he argues by implication that Christianity itself stands innocent before the bar of Roman authority.

In B. Byrne's reflection on Jesus as Messiah in Luke, he argues that while Luke presents Jesus as a Davidic Messiah, the evangelist at key points in his Gospel qualifies that title as it applies to Jesus – given the popular political expectations that the Davidic Messiah would have been expected to free the people from the Romans. Byrne summarises Luke's presentation:

> Though he (Jesus) may have been crucified by a Roman governor as a dangerous political rebel inspired by messianic delusions, this is a total misrepresentation created by his enemies, as the governor himself several times acknowledged. He was a leader who abjured violence and sought to bring peace; the movement gathered in his name and impelled by his Spirit is a movement of conversion and salvation, prophetically critical of, but not fundamentally hostile to, the prevailing civic authority and order. In Luke's view, as I read it, the effective communication of this view was essential to the "assured" establishment of Christian (especially Gentile-Christian) identity (1:4) and to the success of the gospel in the wider Greco-Roman world.[3]

Luke, the great apologist for the Christian movement, is the only writer in the New Testament who is not a Jew. He was not a disciple of Jesus – he tells us, in the opening paragraph of his Gospel, that he gathers his information from those who were eyewitnesses and ministers of the word: these unidentified people are his declared source. Like the other three canonical Gospels, the third Gospel is anonymous; but when people began to wonder about the identity of the Gospel writers, the anonymity was quickly lifted in favour of inspired guesses. According to ancient church tradition, the Luke who appears in Philemon verse 24 as Paul's fellow-worker and is called "the beloved physician" in Colossians 4:14 is the author of the third Gospel. Irenaeus describes Luke as Paul's "inseparable" collaborator,[4] an attribution that he based on the "we" passages in Acts.[5] That tradition has been questioned given the difference between Luke's

---

[3] B. Byrne, "Jesus as Messiah in the Gospel of Luke: Discerning a Pattern of Correction", *Catholic Biblical Quarterly*, 65 (2003), 95.

[4] Irenaeus, *Adversus Haereses*, 3.14.1.

[5] See Acts 16:10-17; 20:5 – 21:18; 27:1 – 28:16.

portrait of Paul and the figure that emerges from Paul's own letters, although that question is largely an issue with Acts and the Pauline letters. That said, however, Luke, like Paul, has particular interest in the abiding truth that Jesus is for everyone: the third evangelist declares early in his Gospel that Jesus comes not only as the glory of the house of Israel, but as the light to enlighten the Gentiles (Luke 2:32).

As Matthew's audience was composed of Jewish and Gentile Christians, Luke's audience seems to be largely Gentile in origin: unlike Matthew and John, Luke does not wrestle with the question of Jewish Christians who have been rejected or expelled by their parent group; neither does he betray an attitude of hostility to the Jews as an active opponent of the emerging Church. This can be seen at the beginning of his writing and also at the end. In Luke's infancy narrative, unlike Matthew's, all his Jewish characters welcome the new things God is revealing in the person of Jesus – there is no confused Joseph, no reluctant wise men of Judea, no murderous King of the Jews, no slaughter of Jewish infants, no forced exile from a Jewish homeland, and no diversion from a dangerous Judea. Instead of Matthew's Gentile magi as the first visitors to the child Jesus, Luke has local shepherds from the surrounding area who are the first evangelists of this new event (Luke 2:18). Luke closes his writing with a more nuanced scene, which includes Jewish acceptance and scepticism. The final narrative scene in the Acts of the Apostles, just before the epilogue, is set in the rented lodging of Paul in Rome, where a large number of Jews come to visit Paul to hear him speak. After Paul spends the day trying to persuade them about Jesus – "some were convinced by what he said, while others disbelieved" (Acts 28:24) – Paul's final appeal is that the salvation he preaches has been sent to the pagans, who will listen to it. The fact that the pagans are listening to the message, rather than the Jews who are rejecting it, is the principal human motivation for the Gentile mission.

Over all this there is the providential plan of God, revealing that Jesus will be a revelation to the Gentiles as well as the glory of his people Israel (Luke 2:32): this central revelation binds the period of Israel, the period of Jesus, and the period of the Church's missionary outreach.

As the first Gentile to write a defence of the Jesus story to the Gentile world, Luke argues an eloquent case on behalf of those who have come to be known as Christians. Writing at a time when Judaism is regarded as a legal religion within the Roman Empire while Christianity is not, Luke will connect Jesus to the history of Israel. He will argue that the Roman perception is profoundly illogical: if the parent (Judaism) is rightly regarded as legal, how can the child that emerged from its womb be dismissed as illegal? In his Gospel Luke presents a seamless continuity between the old story of Israel and the new story of Israel told in the life and ministry of Jesus, and developed in the story of the Church. Where Matthew deals with a story of continuity-discontinuity in Jewish–Christian relations, Luke celebrates a story of seamless continuity.

Table 4.1: **Seamless continuity through three periods**[6]

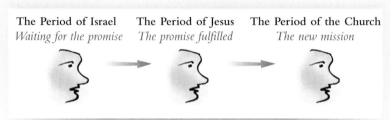

The Period of Israel	The Period of Jesus	The Period of the Church
Waiting for the promise	*The promise fulfilled*	*The new mission*

Luke writes from the Period of the Church and assures Theophilus and others like him that what the Church is doing and preaching is rooted in the Period of Jesus. God's salvation, first revealed in the Period of Israel, is fulfilled in the mission of Jesus of Nazareth. For Luke, Christianity is the natural and logical outcome of Judaism. Among the evangelists Luke is unique in insisting that "the God of Abraham and of Isaac and of Jacob, the God of our fathers" (Acts 3:13) is the one who glorified his servant Jesus and raised him from the dead (Acts 3:15). In his two-volume work Luke writes a story of continual biblical history through the three periods. Luke stresses the connection and continuity between Judaism and Christianity. As Joseph Fitzmyer observes:

> Luke is concerned to show that Christianity, which is rooted in Judaism by the birth of its founder to Jewish parents and by the mark of the covenant (circumcision) has as much right to recognition as a lawful religion in the Roman empire as Judaism itself. It is the logical continuation of Judaism.[7]

So long as Christians were identified with the Jews – easily done since Jesus and all the first Christians were Jewish – they could enjoy the concessions Jews had won from the Roman emperors. When Christians were identified as different from Jews, they could no longer shelter behind the protection afforded to Judaism. Thus they were open to the charges of

---

[6] See H. Conzelmann, *The Theology of Saint Luke* (London: Faber & Faber, 1969), 150.
[7] J. Fitzmyer, *The Gospel According to Luke (I-IX)* (New York: Doubleday, 1983), 10.

social disruption and political disloyalty because they did not want to engage in normal patriotic duties, which included participation in Roman festivals and worship of pagan deities (Jews were excused these provided they prayed for the emperor).

If you notice Luke's architectural structure, he uses the first two chapters of the Gospel to connect the new story of Jesus to the old story of Israel; and he uses the first two chapters of the Acts to connect the new story of the Church to the completed story of Jesus. As Jesus, the protagonist in the Gospel, is pictured as an observant Jew – even from infancy – so Luke will present Paul, the protagonist in the Acts of the Apostles. For example, in Paul's defence speech in Hebrew before the Temple crowd in Jerusalem, he asserts: "I am a Jew, born in Tarsus in Cilicia, but brought up in this city at the feet of Gamaliel, educated strictly according to our ancestral law, being zealous for God, just as all of you are today" (Acts 22:3).[8] Like Jesus, Paul is at home in Judaism; like Jesus, Paul is totally faithful to the Law and the prophets: neither of these men are defectors from the faith of their ancestors. Luke's sustained argument throughout Luke-Acts will be that Christianity's co-founders are upright observant Jews: this new movement is not a protest movement against Judaism but is rooted in the past of Israel and, moreover, is its divinely ordained fulfilment.

One way of looking at the structure of the opening of Luke's Gospel – the infancy narrative – is Luke's depiction of this beginning as one that emerges naturally from Israel: ancient Israel, represented by the Temple piety of old people who have waited for God's promise (Zechariah, Elizabeth, Simeon, Anna) and are now connected to the new people God has chosen, recognising in them the fulfilment of the promises that have directed not only the life of Israel but also their own. I have tried to demonstrate this in Table 4.2.

---

[8] For a reflection of Luke's portrait of Paul, see M.E. Rosenblatt, *Paul the Accused: His Portrait in the Acts of the Apostles* (Minnesota: Liturgical Press, 1995).

Table 4.2

STORY OF OLD ISRAEL	STORY OF NEW ISRAEL
Birth Annunciations	
Place is Judea, in Temple	Place is Galilee, in Nazareth
Parents are introduced:	Parents are introduced:
Zechariah (a priest)	Joseph (of the house of David)
Elizabeth (old and barren)	Mary (a young virgin)
The son is introduced and named:	The son is introduced and named:
John: great before the Lord	Jesus: great: Son of God
Sign: Zechariah is silenced	Sign: old kinswoman is pregnant
The Visitation	
Elizabeth as mother/sign	Mary travels to Judah
Response of blessing:	Response of the Magnificat:
"mother of my Lord"	"Almighty has done great..."
The Birth of the Children	
Birth of John	Birth of Jesus
Joy over the birth	Joy over the birth
(neighbours and relatives)	(angels and shepherds)
Circumcision and Naming	
John is circumcised and named	Jesus is circumcised and named
Response of the Benedictus	
Hidden life of John the Baptist	
Lives in wilderness until he appears to Israel	
The Presentation in the Temple	
← LAW ←	
Temple in Jerusalem	Joseph, Mary and Jesus
Simeon waits to see	"Christ the Lord"
→ SPIRIT →	
"glory of people Israel"	"light to enlighten Gentiles"
Simeon prophesies about child	"sign destined for rejection"
Old Anna speaks about child	"deliverance of Jerusalem"
	Hidden life of Jesus
Conflict in the Temple	
Temple – passover	The parents and Jesus
Jesus stays in the Temple	Parents look among relatives
He questions doctors of the Law	Parents question Jesus
Doctors astounded by intelligence	Parents don't understand
	Hidden life of Jesus

As John the Baptist emerges from the womb of old Israel, coming as an answer to the prayers of the old couple, Jesus will emerge from the womb of a young virgin, coming not as an answer to her prayers but as the new creation of God. In having the two mothers related to one another, Luke underscores the relationship between the two periods: Judaism and Christianity are not mutually exclusive and foreign to one another; rather, the old and the new are united in mutual recognition and reverence. The two mothers together are an eloquent symbol for the whole of Luke's infancy narrative: they wait *together* for the promises of the Lord to be fulfilled in each of them. Finally, the studied parallelism between the birth and childhood of John the Baptist and Jesus, which makes up the body of the infancy narrative, serves to deepen the connection between Israel and Christianity, a connection that culminates in the scene where Jesus is seen at home in the Temple among the doctors of the Law.

The preface

Luke opens his Gospel with a formal literary preface, constructed in one sentence. Unlike Mark in his opening verse, Luke does not call his writing "gospel" but rather "an orderly account" (*diēgēsis,* Luke 1:1) – a term that was often used in classical Hellenistic literature to refer to historical writing. In his preface Luke presents himself as a third-generation Christian: he did not witness the original events themselves like those who were eyewitnesses; he follows a second generation of those who were ministers of the word, including the apostolic preachers, some of whom would also have been eyewitnesses – see Peter's condition for being numbered among the twelve in Acts 1:21-22, where those who were eyewitnesses of the original events now become witnesses to the meaning of these events. Thus stage one in the Gospel formation (the events that were witnessed by Jesus' followers) and stage two (the reflection on those events in the preaching of the apostolic Church) leads now to stage three (a further reflection by those who commit the tradition to writing).[9]

A glance at the opening lines of Josephus' two-volume work *Against Apion* shows a remarkable resemblance to Luke's opening lines in the preface of the Gospel and Acts. Published in the last years of Josephus' life, towards the end of the first century, it is an apologetic defence of Judaism against a wave of anti-Semitism emanating from Alexandria. The opening lines of Josephus' first volume read:

> In my history of our *Antiquities,* most excellent Epaphroditus, I have, I think, made sufficiently clear to any who may peruse that work the

---

[9] For a brief summary of the three stages of Gospel formation, see D. McBride, *The Gospel of Mark: A Reflective Commentary* (Dublin: Dominican Publications, 1996), 7-14.

extreme antiquity of our Jewish race, the purity of the original stock and the manner in which it established itself in the country which we occupy today... Since, however, I observe that a considerable number of persons discredit the statements in my history concerning our antiquity... I consider it my duty to devote a brief treatise to all these points, in order at once to convict our detractors of malignity and deliberate falsehood, to correct the ignorance of others, and to instruct all who desire to know the truth concerning the antiquity of our race.

Josephus' second volume opens in a similar way:

In the first volume of this work, my most esteemed Epaphroditus, I demonstrated the antiquity of our race, corroborating my statements by the writings of the Phoenicians, Chaldaeans, and Egyptians... I also challenged the statements of Manetho, Chaeremon and some others.

Clearly Luke's apologetic defence of Christianity follows the literary fashion of his day in these opening sentences, demonstrating from the outset, like Josephus, the named person his work is dedicated to, the occasion and the purpose of the writing. Like Josephus, Luke wants to set the record straight about his subject matter by outlining the truth as he perceives it: although many others have drawn up accounts of these events, Luke has decided to write his own orderly account following his research of the whole story so that Theophilus and his readers "may know the truth concerning the things of which you have been informed" (1:4). Luke sees himself belonging to an already established tradition of writers, a chain of transmission, and like a dutiful historian who has done comprehensive study based not only on the experience of eyewitnesses and the reflections of preachers but on the writers who have preceded him, he now recommends the fruit of his two-volume research to his audience.

Unlike John's Prologue, Luke steadfastly remains on the level of human history, grounding and securing the narrative as an account of "the things which have been accomplished among us" (1:1). While we would tend to say "the things that have happened among us", Luke betrays his theological outlook that what has happened is a fulfilment of God's plan of salvation. This plan is reflected not in speculative thinking but in historical reality: thus Luke will root his narrative in history, connecting it to:

Roman history

Jesus' birth is linked to the decree of Caesar Augustus when he ordered the census of the Roman world; this happened during the governorship of Quirinius (2:1-2). The appearance of John the Baptist and the beginning of Jesus' ministry is dated as the fifteenth year of Emperor Tiberius' reign (AD 28-29) and with the prefecture of Pontius Pilate (3:1). In the Acts of the Apostles, Luke connects what is happening in the early Christian community with the famine in the days of Emperor Claudius (Acts 11:28) and with Claudius' expulsion of Jews from Rome (Acts 18:2).

Palestinian history

The birth of Jesus is connected with Palestinian history in dating it within the reign of King Herod the Great (Luke 1:5). The ministry of John the Baptist and Jesus is dated to the time of the high priesthood of Annas and Caiaphas, to the reigns of Herod Antipas, tetrarch of Galilee, and Herod Philip, tetrarch of Iturea and Trachonitis (Luke 3:1-2).

Church history

Luke is the only evangelist who connects the Period of Israel and the Period of Jesus to the Period of the emerging Church and its mission in the story of the Acts of the Apostles. Again, the progress of this movement is rooted in history ("for this was not done in a corner", Acts 26:26) and in the story of a community struggling to find its place in a Roman world.

It is to the Gentile world of the Roman Empire that Luke writes his narrative. He dedicates his work to *kratiste Theophile* – "most excellent Theophilus" – an otherwise unknown person whose name appears again in the first verse of Acts. Although Theophilus is not necessarily Luke's patron or publisher,[10] neither is it necessary to argue that the name, which means "beloved of God", is a symbolic designation for Luke's readers. It seems more reasonable to suppose that Theophilus was a real person, one of some influence and standing in the Roman world, not least because the way Luke addresses him is similar to the way Luke has characters in the Acts of the Apostles address the Roman procurators Felix (Acts 23:26; 24:2) and Festus (Acts 26:25). Whoever Theophilus was – either a catechumen under instruction or a well-disposed figure of authority who had heard the incriminating rumours that circulated about Christians – Luke dedicates his great apologia of Christianity to him, and, by extension, to all readers who wish to be informed of the truth of what has

---

[10] See E.J. Goodspeed, "Some Greek Notes: Was Theophilus Luke's Publisher?", *Journal of Biblical Literature*, 73 (1954), 84.

been accomplished in the midst of history. As Edward Ellis comments, "The emphasis upon the 'truth' or 'certainty' of the teaching presupposes denials or heretical perversions of it."[11] More importantly, it presupposes what we know to be the historical suppression and vilification of that truth by the Roman authorities. While the truth that Luke defends is gaining a growing number of adherents among Gentiles, it still remains a truth that is outlawed in the Roman world. Luke's writing to Theophilus to set the record straight about the story of Christianity and its founder is one that corresponds with the transparent apologetic character of the Gospel.

The annunciation of the birth of John

From Luke's elegant rhetorical style in the preface, reflecting the traditional custom of secular writing as he recommends his narrative to his readers, the evangelist moves into biblical language and imagery as he sets his first scene in the Davidic city of Jerusalem, in the priestly court of the Temple. In two sentences we are catapulted from Greco-Roman tradition into Jewish religion, effectively into pre-Christian history. And Luke will now demonstrate how the Christian story is rooted in the Period of Israel, one that can be seen at its best through the artistic literary parallels in the diptych of the two annunciation stories.

Table 4.3

Annunciation of John's birth	Annunciation of Jesus' birth
a) The parents are introduced, expecting no child because of age/barrenness (1:5-7)	a) The parents are introduced, expecting no child because not married (1:26-27)
b) Angel appears in sacred space (v. 11)	b) Angel appears in ordinary space (v. 28)
c) Zechariah is troubled (12)	c) Mary is troubled (29)
d) Angel says: Do not fear . . . (13)	d) Angel says: Do not fear . . . (30)
e) Your wife will bear a son (13)	e) You will bear a son (31)
f) He shall be great before the Lord (15)	f) He shall be great (32)
g) Question: How shall I know this? (18)	g) Question: How shall this be? (34)
h) Answer: I have been sent to announce this (19)	h) Answer: Holy Spirit will come upon you (35)
i) Sign given: You shall be mute (20)	i) Sign given: Aged cousin has conceived (36)
j) Zechariah's imposed silence (22)	j) Mary's spontaneous response (38)
k) Zechariah went away (23)	k) The angel went away (38)

[11] E. Ellis, *The Gospel of Luke* (London: Oliphants, 1974), 68.

Luke situates his story in the days of King Herod, who ruled over Palestine from 37 until 4 BC. The first characters to be introduced in the Gospel story are from the Period of Israel, an old married couple from the country (v.39): a priest called Zechariah, a name which means, "The Lord remembers", and his wife, Elizabeth. Both belong to the tribe of Aaron, all the male members of which were priests – interestingly the only Elizabeth mentioned in the Old Testament is Elisheba, the wife of Aaron the high priest (Exodus 6:23). Before he mentions the childlessness of the couple, Luke states unambiguously that they are upright people who scrupulously observe the Law; he describes them in terms used of the *anawim*, the faithful remnant of God, and this glowing description avoids the charge that barrenness was an affliction which God visited on sinful people (Leviticus 20:20).

The whole atmosphere of this narrative is built around the perception that John the Baptist emerges from the Old Testament: he is the last of the great prophets of Israel; he is born of aged and pious parents, both of priestly stock, who represent all that is good in their observance of the Law and in Temple piety. As E. Franklin observes: "Law, Temple, and prophecy together were to produce John who, while yet in the womb, would acknowledge his Lord and witness to him (1:44)."[12]

Both husband and wife are advanced in years, which explains why the couple cannot have children now, but Luke includes the additional note that Elizabeth was barren. The couple is doubly incapacitated, and there seems no human ground for hope. The situation of the couple is not hopeless, however, given the history of the people of God. In the Old Testament, Sarah, Rebekah, Rachel, Hannah and the mother of Samson were all barren; but their barrenness was no barrier to the promise and the plan of God. God's plan is not hindered by barren wombs and old age: paradoxically, these become grounds of new hope and possibility, and for the birth of famous men in the history of Israel. The birth of John is firmly set within that great tradition of Israel.

If Matthew opens his Gospel with the name of Abraham as he begins the genealogy of Jesus, Luke opens his Gospel with the retelling of the story of Abraham. There are only two instances in the whole Bible where a couple is incapable of having children because they are both old and the wife is barren: Abraham and Sarah; Zechariah and Elizabeth. Pushing back their reflection on the beginning of the Jesus story to the patriarch Abraham is something that both Matthew and Luke achieve in their different ways, effectively rooting the origins of the Jesus story in the

---

[12] E. Franklin, "Luke", in J. Barton and J. Muddiman (eds), *The Oxford Bible Commentary* (New York: Oxford University Press, 2001), 926.

Period of Israel. The primary patriarchal pattern for the birth story of John is clearly the birth story of Isaac (Genesis 17): the announcement of the promise is made to an old man, who reacts to the presence of the supernatural with fear and awe; he is told that his wife will give birth to a male child, what name to call the child, and how the child will distinguish himself in his future life. Objections are made, but the visionary is given a sign to reassure him of the reality of the promise. Later, there is joy surrounding the birth itself (Genesis 21:6; Luke 1:58).

The setting for Luke's opening story is the Temple, where he will also bring his Gospel to a close (24:53). The priests who officiated at the morning and afternoon sacrifice in the Temple were divided into twenty-four groups, each group serving twice a year for a week at a time (see 1 Chronicles 24:1-9). There were so many priests in service – Jeremias estimates that there were eighteen thousand priests and Levites in the Palestine of Jesus' day[13] – that it was a rare privilege for a priest to officiate, an honour which happened only once in his lifetime if he were fortunate. Four officiating priests were needed each day: one to make the burnt animal offering, one to make the meal offering, one to maintain the candlestick; it is a very special day for Zechariah because he has won the fourth lot – the prize – to burn incense in the sanctuary for the afternoon service at the ninth hour, 3 pm.

He enters the sanctuary next to the Holy of Holies to offer incense, a symbol of the prayer of the people who are outside making their petitions to God. The angel appears to Zechariah who is fearful – a normal human reaction in the face of the supernatural. The angel counsels him not to be afraid, for his prayer has been heard – both his personal prayer and priestly prayer, because his son will come as an answer to parents' longings and an answer to Israel's hopes (Luke 1:16). The angel announces a canticle of joy, which situates the origins and mission of John as clearly continuous with God's saving actions in the course of Israel's history: following that tradition John "will turn many of the sons of Israel to the Lord their God" (1:16). John will play a key transitional role: in Luke's story of seamless continuity between the Period of Israel, the Period of Jesus, and the Period of the Church, John emerges in this narrative from the Period of Israel; he is last of Israel's prophets: "The Law and the Prophets were until John; since then the Good News of the kingdom of God is preached" (16:16). As an adult, in the wilderness of Judea, he will inaugurate the Period of Jesus. Thus it makes sense for Luke in composing this overture to his Gospel that John will be the precursor of Jesus at the beginning of his life as he will be his precursor in the public ministry.

---

[13] J. Jeremias, *Jerusalem in the Time of Jesus* (Philadelphia: Fortress, 1969), 198-204.

The angel assures Zechariah that the birth of John will bring joy and gladness to many – not just to his parents – and he then outlines the future career of John. Even before he emerges from his mother's womb, John will be filled with the Holy Spirit which will help him to bring back many of the people of Israel to God. In the spirit of Elijah (Malachi 4:5-6), John will lead a movement of conversion to God and prepare the people for the Lord.

After hearing this astounding announcement, Zechariah reacts cautiously, and, exactly as Abraham did before God (Genesis 17:17), kindly reminds the supernatural visitor about the practical limitations of old age. To Zechariah's objection, "I am an old man..." the angel counters with, "I am Gabriel, who stand in the presence of God." Zechariah is concerned with human problems while the angel focuses on the power of God. Zechariah's request and disbelief are answered with a punitive sign: he will be dumb until the angel's word has been accomplished. Just when Zechariah has some good news to announce he is punished by not being able to declare it to anyone.

The people are waiting for the priestly blessing – the encounter with the angel has unavoidably delayed the old priest. When the priest emerged from the sanctuary, he was required to give a blessing over the people (Numbers 6:21-27), but Zechariah cannot pronounce the blessing; through the signs he makes, however, the people, somewhat curiously, understand he has seen a vision. After the time of his group's service in the Temple, Zechariah returns home. As an epilogue to the story, Luke adds that some time later Elizabeth does conceive – like Sarah without herself receiving an annunciation – and, for five months, keeps to herself. The secrecy of Elizabeth's confinement will play its part in the next episode: when the angel announces to Mary the news that her kinswoman is now in her sixth month (Luke 1:36), Mary learns of this for the first time, so the information acts as an effective sign of the new things that God is doing in the midst of people.

The annunciation of the birth of Jesus

In placing the annunciation to Mary "in the sixth month" and having Gabriel named as the messenger, Luke binds these two annunciation stories together. As the first annunciation was set in the sacred space of the Temple, the annunciation to Mary takes place in ordinary space, in the town of Nazareth, where Mary lives and is betrothed to a man called Joseph, of the house of David. Luke will later trace the genealogy of Jesus through Joseph to David (3:23-31). The Jewish marriage consisted of two distinct stages: betrothal in the exchange of consent before witnesses, and then, usually after an interval of about a year, the groom would formally take the bride to his family home. Even though she remained for some time in her own family home after betrothal, the girl was legally considered to be a wife since the Jewish law regarded betrothal as a binding contract which could be broken only by divorce. As Eduard Schweizer notes: "Virgins who lost their betrothed before marriage were considered widows."[14]   Mary has gone through the first stage of the marriage and is betrothed to Joseph, but she has not yet moved in to live with him. She is still a virgin.

In the annunciation of Jesus' birth, Luke presents Jesus as superior to John: John will be the one who will prepare the people for the Lord; Jesus will be the one who will rule, and "of his kingdom there will be no end". Although involving divine intervention, John was conceived in a human manner, and was filled with the Holy Spirit while still in the womb. That manner of divine intervention is clearly attested elsewhere in the Jewish Bible. While John is filled with the Holy Spirit from his mother's womb, the Holy Spirit is directly involved in the *conception* of Jesus, and comes upon Jesus' mother. Jesus is conceived in a way entirely appropriate to such a new creation – an unprecedented virginal conception through the power of the Holy Spirit, which points to his unique status as the Davidic Messiah and the Son of God.

If both annunciation stories clearly stand in the literary tradition of biblical annunciations of birth in the Old Testament, what distinguishes this annunciation story from all the other narratives is Mary's virginal conception and the unique greatness of the child.[15] A virginal conception has no precedence in Jewish thought, and the arguments that Luke is influenced by Greek pagan legends remain powerfully unconvincing. Brown argues to the appropriateness of the virginal conception from a comparison of the two annunciation accounts in Luke:

> In the JBap annunciation, when he introduces the two parents (1:7), Luke tells us of the human difficulty in their lives that prevents conception; and it is precisely that difficulty which is resumed in Zechariah's "How" objection to the angel in 1:18. In the Jesus annunciation, when he introduces Mary (1:27), Luke mentions twice that she is a virgin; and it is that factor which is resumed in Mary's "How" objection to the angel in 1:34: "I have had no relations with a man." If the age and barrenness of Zechariah and

[14] E. Schweizer, *The Good News According to Luke*, trans. David E. Green (London: SPCK, 1984), 27.

[15] For a comparison of biblical annunciation stories, see the tables in R.E. Brown, *The Birth of the Messiah* (London: Chapman, 1993) 156, 248, 297.

Elizabeth were divinely overcome in the conception of JBap, the human difficulty of the virginity of Mary must be overcome by divine power in the conception of Jesus.[16]

If Luke is emphatic in his identification of Mary as a virgin, his only identification of Joseph is no less important, namely, that he is "of the House of David". After King David conquered the Jebusite city of Jerusalem – which was not strongly identified with any tribe and could, therefore, serve as a neutral capital – he expressed the desire to bring the exiled ark back to Jerusalem and build a house for it (see 2 Samuel 7). After the triumphant return of the ark to the City of David, Nathan the prophet hears of David's regret that while he as king lives in a house of cedar, God dwells in a tent: hence David's plan to build God a house. That night Nathan receives instructions from God to command David not to build him a house; instead God will build David a house (dynasty), assuring him that he would have a descendant on the throne in perpetuity, and, using the language of divine adoption, that his son would be God's son. That covenant to David is incorporated into the text of the angel's annunciation to Mary:

Table 4.4

2 Samuel 7	Luke 1
[9]"I will make for you a *great* name...	[32a]"He will be *great* ... be called *Son* of the Most High;
[13]"I will establish *the throne* of *his kingdom* for ever	[32b]and the Lord God will give him *the throne* of *his father* David,
[14]"I will be *his father,* and he shall be *my* son...	[33a]and he will reign over the *house* of Jacob for *ever;*
[16]"And your *house* and your *kingdom* shall be made sure for ever..."	[33b]and of his kingdom there will be no end."

---

[16] Brown, *The Birth of the Messiah,* 301.

In this first declaration of Jesus' status, there can be no stronger way of rooting the figure of Jesus in the Period of Israel than identifying him as the son of David, heir of God's unique promise to King David. By this Luke secures his argument that the founder of Christianity emerges from Israel, that Christianity is born out of Judaism. Although the original promise referred to an ongoing line rather than an individual, the psalms tended to apply it to a specific individual king (Psalm 2:7; 110:4), an understanding which was later interpreted to apply to a messianic figure. Jesus will be the promised inheritor of David's throne, and he will rule "over the house of Jacob forever" – that is, Israel.

Luke moves from asserting Jesus' Davidic status to the second and more important declaration of Jesus' status – given as an answer to Mary's "How?" question – that he will be the Son of the Most High. In Paul's letter to the Romans (written about AD 55-57) he tells the community that he has been set apart for preaching the Gospel of God, and defines that Gospel by using an older formula that would have been known to this community:

> The gospel concerning his Son, who was descended from David according to the flesh and was declared to be *Son of God* with *power* according to the *spirit* of holiness by resurrection from the dead (Romans 1:3-4).

Paul moves from the Davidic identification of Jesus to his status as Son of God, a pattern that Luke follows in his narrative, except that now Jesus' status as Son of God is attached not to his resurrection from the dead but to his conception into life. The three key terms associated with Jesus' identity, however, noted in italics in the above quotation, are also pressed back by Luke to the conception:

> The Holy *Spirit* will come upon you, and the *power* of the Most High will overshadow you; therefore the child to be born will be called holy, the *Son of God* (Luke 1:35).

In Luke's theology, the child will be called holy, the Son of God, from his conception. Luke's theology does not include a pre-incarnational Christology, and it seems from this verse that he sees the power of the Holy Spirit bringing the Son of God into existence. The recognition of Jesus as the Son of God, first applied to Jesus in the pre-Gospel period as one associated with the *resurrection*,[17] is now pressed back, as in Matthew, to the moment of conception. While Mark pressed it back to the story of

---

[17] See, for example, Acts 2:32. 36; 5:31; 13:32-33; Romans 1:3-4; Philippians 2:8-9.

the baptism, during which Jesus' identity as Son of God is announced to the readers of his Gospel, John will press it back further to pre-existing the beginning of the world. Wherever the evangelists begin the story – on the banks of the river Jordan (Mark), with the conception of Jesus (Matthew and Luke), before the beginning of creation (John) – each evangelist in turn will announce the identity of Jesus. In that sense, Luke is consistent with his brother evangelists in sharing his Christology, his understanding of the identity of Jesus, at the beginning of his narrative.

Having established for the reader the glorious identity of this child and his future accomplishments, Luke moves on to the next literary stage of the annunciation narrative in the hearer's objection and offer of a sign. Elizabeth's pregnancy is not yet public knowledge for she has hidden herself, but Gabriel now tells Mary that her relative, who was both old and barren, is now six months pregnant. When God asked Abraham why Sarah laughed at the promise of her pregnancy, God put the question: "Is anything too hard for the Lord?" (Genesis 18:14). That question is now clearly answered by God's messenger, "For with God nothing will be impossible" (Luke 1:37).

Mary's response is unparalleled in the other annunciation narratives: she is the one who when hearing the word of God gladly allows that word to form her life. Later, her son will say during his public ministry: "My mother and my brethren are those who hear the word of God and do it" (8:19-21). Mary is now presented as the perfect disciple who is a hearer of the word (*rhēma*) and a doer of the word. With that response, the angel takes his leave. Thus, Mary becomes the literal embodiment of the promise of God: she conceives the promise, she becomes pregnant with the promise, and she will give birth to the promise. And the promise will be called "holy, the Son of God".

The visitation

As one day Jesus will travel south from Nazareth to see John the Baptist in the wilderness of Judea, so the mother of Jesus now travels south to a town in the hills of Judea to see the mother of John the Baptist. Luke's account of Mary's visitation to Elizabeth brings together the two mothers who have been promised birth through divine intervention. Mary hurries to the home of her relative, Elizabeth, whom she greets and brings out of her seclusion. At the sound of her greeting, the babe in Elizabeth's womb leaps for joy (see the leaping of the twins in Rachel's womb in Genesis 25:22). Mary has already received a revelation from Gabriel of what God has done for her relative; now Elizabeth, because of the movement of another messenger, is inspired to recognise what God has done for Mary. Luke has already stated how John would be filled with the Holy Spirit even from his mother's womb (1:15) and how he *would* prepare people for the Lord (1:17); now Luke shows how the unborn prophet recognises the greatness of the unborn Lord, and moves his mother to recognise the presence of her Lord in Mary. Much later, John will be uncertain whether Jesus really is the promised one (7:19); but now is the moment for womb-shaking rejoicing, appropriate to the beginning of the messianic era.

Filled with the Holy Spirit, Elizabeth expresses her joy in a canticle praising Mary. She acclaims Mary as blessed (*eulogēmenē*): strictly speaking, Elizabeth is not conferring a blessing on Mary, but joyfully acknowledging that Mary is already blessed by God: "Blessed are you (by God) among women". The double blessing recognises that Mary is blessed precisely because the fruit of her womb is blessed. Elizabeth goes on to indicate her own unworthiness that the mother of "my Lord" should visit her, and explains that she knew Mary was indeed the mother of her *Kyrios* because of the movement of her unborn child in response to Mary's greeting. Elizabeth's canticle comes to a close in a final beatitude in which she rejoices in something more important than Mary's physical motherhood: in her faithful obedience in believing that the word of God would find fulfilment in her.

The priority that Elizabeth gives to Mary's faith over her physical motherhood is reflected later in Jesus' public ministry, when a woman from the crowd will call out a beatitude: "Blessed is the womb that bore you and the breasts that nursed you!" (Luke 11:27) – focusing on the physical act of motherhood that has produced such a son. Jesus will reply with another beatitude: "Blessed rather are those who hear the word of God and obey it!" (11:28; see 8:21). Jesus' beatitude does not negate that of the woman in the crowd; rather, as a corrective, it gives prime importance, like Elizabeth's beatitude, to faithful obedience to the word of God. Elizabeth's husband, who did not believe in the inherent power of the word of God, is now overshadowed by the young mother who is blessed because she believed that God's word would indeed be accomplished in her.

In her canticle Elizabeth praised Mary for being mother of the Lord and for her faith; now, Mary responds by praising God in a hymn of gladness. In the course of his infancy narrative, Luke presents the reader with three substantial canticles of praise, the Magnificat, the Benedictus and the

Nunc Dimittis, which he attributes to Mary, Zechariah and Simeon, respectively – the Latin names are taken from the Vulgate, the authorised version of the medieval Church. Luke portrays the three speakers as representative figures of the *anawim*, the faithful remnant of Israel who put their complete trust and hope in God. The three canticles which they speak are equally representative of the hopes and longings of the *anawim*.

Most scholars would agree that none of the speakers actually composed the canticles ascribed to them – not least because they have a somewhat tenuous connection to the specific context in which they are placed. It would appear that Luke has taken old compositions of poetry from the Greek Old Testament (Septuagint) which proclaimed the saving action of God, and applied their general sentiments to the occasion of the speakers in his Gospel. In composition and in outlook, the canticles are Jewish rather than Christian, and closely parallel the psalms and hymns written in the first and second centuries BC.[18] The parallels are clear in 1 Maccabees – which has led Winter to argue that the Magnificat and the Benedictus were originally Maccabean psalms.[19] Whatever their specific origin, it would seem that Luke did not compose them.

The Magnificat is an echo of the canticle of Hannah who voiced her prayer in thanksgiving for the Lord's turning her barrenness into pregnancy (1 Samuel 2:1-10). Since the wording does not specifically reflect what has happened to Mary, some scholars attribute the Magnificat to Elizabeth, arguing that it is more appropriate coming from a woman who has been raised from barrenness; but the manuscript evidence clearly favours Mary as the speaker. Further, since "low estate" does not necessarily refer to barrenness but can be a description of the state of the *anawim*, and since verse 48, which many scholars would see as a Lucan addition, speaks of "handmaid" – a word which Mary uses to describe herself in the annunciation scene (1:38) – the ascription to Mary would seem to make more sense.

The Magnificat is a prayer made from the position of the downtrodden and the poor who praise God for his might, his mercy and his continued concern. The prayer reflects what God has done both for the individual and for the community, which gives the speaker reason to praise God for his attributes of holiness, mercy, strength, care and remembrance of promises. It praises God who is not just a giver of promises but a keeper of promises. It is the prayer of the poor of God who rejoice that littleness has been blessed. In that sense, it is the hymn of a Cinderella people: the proud are toppled from their precious pedestals; the mighty find

---

[18] See the extended discussion in S. Farris, *The Hymns of Luke's Infancy Narratives* (Sheffield: JSOT, 1985).

[19] P. Winter, "Magnificat and Benedictus – Maccabean Psalms?", *Bulletin of the John Rylands Library*, 37 (1954), 328-347.

themselves unemployed; the little people are unimportant no more; the hungry are attended to at last; the rich are solemnly awarded nothing. The Magnificat celebrates the wisdom of reversal and praises the revolution of God – what he has achieved in establishing a kingdom where the forgotten and the lowly are held precious in the sight of God.

If the Magnificat praises God for his concern and testifies to his continuing fidelity, it is equally clear about God's attitude to those who are involved in oppression: they are "scattered", "put down", "sent empty away". No sympathy is given to those who live well because someone somewhere dies of neglect – a theme which Luke will develop throughout the pages of his Gospel. The God of Israel is the God who saves (1:47) and who is actively involved in liberating his people from the powers that oppress them. The prayer speaks of a God who has unambiguous positions on religious, social and economic matters: in that sense, the Magnificat is a revolutionary hymn of praise. Thus Gomá Civit, after a lengthy exegesis of the Magnificat, concludes: "The cry of all the humble and oppressed, of all time and of the present, is recognised in the Mary of the Gospel."[20]

In the conclusion (1:54-55) Luke shows – given that he has ascribed this prayer to Mary – that what has happened to Mary is rooted in the Period of Israel, securing the new things God is accomplishing "according to the promise he made to our ancestors, Abraham and to his descendants for ever". Again the Jesus story is consciously attached to the story of Israel; again the note is reprised that the beginnings of Christianity emerge flawlessly from the history of Israel. Indeed one could see this connection at the heart of the whole scene: in the meeting of the two mothers there is a meeting of the two testaments, Jewish and Christian. The mother of the new Israel journeys to meet a mother of Old Israel, the mother of the last of the great prophets. The two of them are related – Luke is the only evangelist to have Jesus related to John the Baptist – in the same way that the New Testament is related to the Old Testament: indeed Elizabeth recognises Mary as "mother of my Lord" (1:43). In their greeting and recognition, the two testaments celebrate one another.

After the conclusion of Mary's canticle, Luke states that Mary stays with Elizabeth another three months. The time of pregnancy was regarded as ten lunar months, so Luke has Mary depart for home before the birth of John the Baptist. The visitation over, the scene is now clear for the two births, each of which will be recounted in separate birth narratives.

---

[20] I. Gomá Civit, *The Song of Salvation: The Magnificat* (Middlegreen: St Paul, 1986), 106.

The birth and circumcision of John

The stigma of her barrenness removed by divine favour, Elizabeth gives birth to a son. The neighbours and relatives discover the good news after the birth has taken place, and they come to rejoice with Elizabeth that the Lord has looked so kindly on her. The occasion for the gathering is the family ceremony of circumcision, which normally took place eight days after the birth (Genesis 17:12), and the naming of the child, which usually happened immediately after birth. The circumcision will mark John as one who belongs to the people of Israel, heir to the promises, and oblige him eventually to honour the Mosaic Law. As Fitzmyer notes:

> The incorporation of the forerunner of Jesus the Messiah into Israel is important in the Lucan story because of the eventual incorporation of Jesus himself, for Luke will be at pains at the end of his two-volume work to show that Christianity is a logical outgrowth of Judaism. Those who inaugurate it and found it must be shown to be part of Judaism.[21]

There was a tradition in priestly circles to name the child after the grandfather; the expectation in this gathering, however, is to call the new child after his father. Elizabeth intervenes to say that the child will be called John, a name which means "The Lord's gracious gift". The child's name – given by divine mandate rather than chosen by human selection – speaks of his origin and vocation: he comes as a gift from God, and his life will be a gift to God's people. Clearly, Elizabeth is departing from traditional practice for the neighbours remind her that none of her relatives is so called. Since there is no precedent for the name in the family, the gathering appeals to Zechariah by making signs – it appears that he is deaf as well as dumb. Zechariah calls for a writing tablet, which he no doubt kept handy over the recent months, and confirms what his wife has said: since Zechariah was deaf and could not hear what his wife said, the surprise is probably at the unexpected confirmation of the unusual choice. It is possible that Zechariah had used the writing tablet to communicate the name to Elizabeth, but it appears that Luke is telling us that both parents acted, without collusion, under the inspiration of God.

Gabriel had imposed silence on Zechariah "until the day that these things come to pass" (1:20); the promised things have now come to pass and Zechariah's mouth is opened and his tongue is freed. The awe of the neighbours increases an octave when Zechariah speaks again: they are fearful – a traditional Lucan response to a supernatural event. The unusual events which accompanied the circumcision and naming of John drive

---

[21] Fitzmyer, *The Gospel According to Luke (I-IX)*, 376.

those who witnessed them to carry the story to others. So, the tale of these marvellous events is spread around the hill country, and those who hear the story cherish it and ask themselves about the future role of this child. It is only after Luke ushers the neighbours off the literary scene that he inserts the canticle of Zechariah.

When Zechariah finds his voice again, he does not use it to take issue with God or his messenger for the imposed silence which he has had to endure. Zechariah speaks words of blessing and praise and prophecy. The neighbours may speculate about the future of the child, but Zechariah knows what lies in the child's future story, and he will echo that revelation in the canticle.

Some scholars argue to a clear division in the structure of the Benedictus: 1:68-75 in the form of a *beraka* or blessing which praises God for his faithfulness in redeeming his people, and 1:76-79 in the form of a *genethliakon* or birthday hymn made in honour of the new child. Certainly, verses 68-75 are general in tone and repeat the traditional formula of a hymn of praise in first addressing praise to God and then enlisting reasons for that praise – as well as expressing the mentality of the *anawim* as previously set forth in the Magnificat; but given that Luke has adopted a general hymn of praise, as he did with the Magnificat, verses 76-77 can be seen as Luke's addition for the purpose of specifying the future role of John the Baptist in the context of the coming Messiah. These lines answer the neighbours' question about the future of the child. Verses 78-79 are general in tone and can be seen as part of the original hymn. This way of looking at the structure of the canticle sees it as a composite whole, with Luke's insertion in verses 76-77.

Treated as a composite whole the Benedictus can be divided as follows:

Introduction (1:68a) – The canticle opens with Zechariah using a traditional form of blessing God, one which identifies God in his relationship with Israel. The form recalls a familiar psalmic blessing (Psalms 41:13; 72:18; 106:48; also 1 Kings 1:48).

First Stanza (1:68b-71) – The primary reason for praising God is because "he has visited his people". As with 1:51ff the verb is in the past tense denoting accomplishment. The visit of God has brought salvation because "he has raised up" a "horn of salvation" (1:69a) in the house of David (1 Samuel 2:1; Psalm 132:16-17; Ezekiel 29:21).

The power of salvation is Jesus who is the Christ (John the Baptist has no links with the house of David). What God has accomplished is what he promised to do by the mouth of his holy prophets (Acts 3:21).

Second Stanza (1:72-75) – The saving work of God is also a fulfilment of the covenant made with Abraham and his descendants (Exodus 2:24; Psalm 106:45; Micah 7:20). The purpose of God's liberating his people was to enable them to serve him in holiness all their days (1 Kings 9:4-5; Joshua 24:14).

Third Stanza (1:76-77) – This Lucan insert into a tapestry of Old Testament texts answers the question, "What then will this child be?" (1:66). In conscious contrast to Jesus who has been designated "Son of the Most High" (1:32) John will be called "Prophet of the Most High" (1:76). He will go before the Lord (1:15, 17) and enable people to experience salvation through the forgiveness of their sins (3:3).

Conclusion (1:78-79) – Previous themes are gathered together in the concluding verses of the canticle. (Manuscripts and therefore scholars are divided on whether the tense of the verb "visit" is past or future: given the recapitulation form of the conclusion it would seem appropriate if it were translated in the past tense.) In his mercy God has visited his people *anatolē ex hypsous* – literally, "a rising from on high" (Isaiah 60:1). Zechariah refers to Jesus as the Messiah, the "Dawn from on High" who will appear to those in darkness (Isaiah 42:6-7) to guide them into the way of peace (Isaiah 59:8).

Central to the proclamation of the Benedictus is the revelation that God has visited his people in the person of Jesus: in verse 68 the action refers to God while in verse 78 it is directly related to the coming of the Messiah. In the Benedictus the visit of God is a messianic concept, and since Jesus has already been identified as the Davidic Messiah (1:32. 33) he summarises in his person the visit of God.

The Greek verb which Luke uses in 1:68. 78 is *episkepsetai*. In secular Greek the verb means "to look upon, to consider, to have regard to something or someone", and when referring to the gods means "graciously to look upon, to care for, to watch over".[22] In the Greek Old Testament the verb is used often to describe what God is doing and has

[22] See H.W. Beyer, "ἐπισκέπτομαι in the New Testament", *Theological Dictionary of the New Testament* II, ed G. Kittel (Grand Rapids: Eerdmans, 1964), 600.

105

variety of connotations: in most cases denoting the active intervention of God in history for the purpose of revealing his will and saving his people. And that action is generally linked to the most important visit of God in the experience of Israel, his saving intervention in Egypt (Exodus 4:31). Luke's use of *episkepsetai* capitalises on its constant use in the Greek Old Testament to refer to the action of God visiting his people, rather than on the secular usage that speaks more of an *attitude* of mind. Among the Gospels the use of the verb to describe the action of God is peculiar to Luke and occurs elsewhere in the New Testament only in Hebrews 2:6. Luke uses it again in 7:16 and Acts 15:14, and the substantive "visitation" in Jesus' lamentation over Jerusalem (Luke 19:44).

Finally, in a brief note testifying to the physical and spiritual growth of John, Luke rounds off this section before moving on to the story of the birth of Jesus. John makes his preparation for his public ministry in the wilderness, the traditional testing ground for the people of God and the prophets. When Luke returns to the story of John, he will continue it where he left it – in the wilderness (3:2).

The birth and circumcision of Jesus

The birth of Jesus (2:6-7), like that of John (1:57-58), is narrated in two verses: John's birth was dated in the days of King Herod of Judea, a local Jewish event, while Jesus' birth is dated during a significant secular enactment of Rome when "a decree went out from Emperor Augustus that all the world should be registered" (2:1) – noting it as a world event. While John's birth is attended by neighbours and relatives, Jesus' birth is attended by shepherds who are summoned miraculously and by a heavenly host of angels. The burden of Luke's birth narrative about Jesus is devoted to the circumstances surrounding the birth (2:1-6) and the story of the shepherds (2:8-20); the narrative concludes with a brief statement about the circumcision of Jesus (2:21). Matthew begins the story of Jesus with his being born in the house of Joseph in Bethlehem; he later transfers the family north to Nazareth by reference to the cruelty of Archelaus who rules over the territory of Judea (Matthew 2:19-23). Luke has the opposite problem of transferring the story from Nazareth in Galilee south to Bethlehem in Judea; for this he uses the device of a census of the Roman world.

Scholars have unresolved questions about the historical accuracy of the events surrounding Luke's birth narrative:

there is no historical record of an empire-wide census in the time of Caesar Augustus;

a Roman census could not have been carried out in Herod's kingdom while Herod was still reigning;

the Roman custom of taxation was based on the individual's place of residence, not his place of ancestry (at a time of census the authorities want people to stay in the same place rather than have a population travelling up and down the country);

Joseph would not have been required to bring Mary with him;

the historian Josephus does refer to a census of Quirinius that was carried out in AD 6/7, one that was without precedent in the region.

Ingenious attempts have been made to resolve the historical difficulties, but the important question which can be answered concerns Luke's theological intentions: the census places the birth of Jesus within the frame of Roman history, during the peaceful reign of Caesar Augustus; it also serves to situate the birth in Joseph's ancestral city, Bethlehem, the place prophesied to mark the beginning of the messianic visit. As importantly, it shows the parents of Jesus as obedient subjects of Rome. As Eugene LaVerdiere notes:

> In light of Luke's general effort to show how Jesus and the Church were just and legitimate in terms of Roman law, the indication is significant. It contributes to the author's apologetic for Roman recognition, an apologetic urgently required to counter the persecutions which were arising in various quarters. In a sense, Luke 2:1-5 is Luke's own appeal to Caesar (see Acts 25:10-12).[23]

The obedience of Jesus' parents to the Roman census, which was carried out for tax purposes by Quirinius in AD 6/7, stands in marked contrast to the violent response of Judas the Galilean and the Zealots who revolted against it, a revolt that eventually led to the Jewish war of independence in AD 66.[24] Luke was certainly aware of Judas' revolt, mentioning it in Acts 5:37. As the new governor of Syria, Quirinius held a census of the population and territory under his supervision. Judas taught the people that to submit to the census was to deny the Lordship of God – Rome had no right either to number God's people or to record ownership of God's land – and he provoked his followers and others to rebel. In contrast to the rebellion of Judas the Galilean, the Galilean

---

[23] E. LaVerdiere, *Luke* (Dublin: Veritas, 1980), 31.

[24] Our main source of information about Judas the Galilean is from Flavius Josephus, *Antiquities* 18.11-6; *Jewish War* 2.8.1.

parents of Jesus are seen as loyal subjects of Rome, carrying out their obligations.

In his birth narrative (2:1-20) Luke gives more attention to the interpretation of Jesus' birth by the angels and the shepherds' visitation than he does to the birth itself. His account of the birth of Jesus is spare and simple: while the couple is in Bethlehem, Mary's time comes; she delivers her first-born, warms him in swaddling cloths and lays him in a manger because there is no room at the inn.

The first thing we are told about the new-born child is that he is wrapped in swaddling cloths, a description that will be given to the shepherds for its value as a sign to bear out the angel's message of the birth of a saviour in David's city (2:12). The detail is not insignificant but has a purpose beyond itself, recalling King Solomon's description of his birth:

> I was nursed with care in swaddling cloths. For no king has had a different beginning of existence; there is for all one entrance into life, and one way out (Wisdom 7:4-6).

Solomon's description of birth astride death, focusing on the detail of the swaddling cloths, is an important one because of who he is: he is a royal child, the son of David. The swaddling cloths, therefore, have the function of a sign because they point not to the poverty of the parents but the royalty of the child. The second point Luke tells us about the child is that he is laid in a manger because there is no room at the inn. Again the detail is important, not least because Luke mentions it three times: in the first instance as the place where Mary lays the child (2:7); secondly, as a sign to the shepherds (v.12); thirdly, as a sign which works its purpose (v.16). The manger as a sign recalls the text from Isaiah:

> The ox knows its owner
> and the ass its master's crib (*phatnē*);
> but Israel does not know [me],
> my people does not understand [me] (1:3).

In the Greek Old Testament the comparison between Israel and God is highlighted by the addition of "me" in the last two lines. (Both the Septuagint and Luke use *phatnē*: manger or crib.) In the text from Isaiah the dumb animals are better at recognising their owner, the source of their nourishment, than the people of Israel are at recognising the visitation of the Lord. The manger, a feeding trough for animals, becomes a symbol for the recognition of the Lord by his people. The fact that the shepherds recognise the manger as a sign of the birth of the saviour is an indication that, unlike the Israel of the past, they do know the manger of their Lord.

The manger stands in deliberate contrast to the inn, and Giblin suggests that the comparison yields more meaning in the light of Jeremiah 14:8 which he literally translates from the Septuagint:

> Why are you like one in the land of an alien, like a traveller (or inhabitant) who lodges in an inn?[25]

Jeremiah's appeal is followed immediately by an oracle of punishment: God states that he accepts his people no longer but will visit them with punishment (Jeremiah 14:10), and reveals that the prophets who announce "assured peace" are not sent by divine command (14:13-14). Jeremiah's plea, addressed to the Lord and saviour of Israel, is answered in Luke's narrative: the saviour does not stay in an inn like an alien who can depend on the kindness of relatives or friends, but is laid in a manger where he is recognised by his own people in the shepherds – whose location is given as "the countryside close by" the city of David (see Micah 5:1-5). And after the manger is given as a sign to the shepherds, there is a proclamation of peace made not by false prophets but by divine messengers commissioned to bring God's revelation as Good News.

The Good News announced to the shepherds is central to Luke's birth narrative: this annunciation now describes Jesus by three christological titles: Saviour, Messiah, and Lord (Luke 2:11). These titles, unlike those describing the royal child in Isaiah 9:6, are born of a resurrection faith which recognises the full significance of Jesus in the light of his exaltation (see Acts 2:36; 5:31). In the same way the canticle of the heavenly host proclaims glory to God in heaven and peace on earth to those whom God favours (Luke 2:14), so later in the Gospel narrative the whole group of disciples will joyfully praise God:

> Blessed is the King who comes
> in the name of the Lord!
> Peace in heaven,
> and glory in the highest heaven (Luke 19:38).

As Brown comments:"The same kind of poetry used to hail Jesus as the Messiah at the end of his ministry is applicable to the birth of the Messiah. But in the present Gospel sequence, Luke is telling us that the angels of

---

[25] C.H. Giblin,"Reflections on the Sign of the Manger", *Catholic Biblical Quarterly*, 29 (1967), 99.

heaven recognised at the beginning of Jesus' life what the disciples came to know only at the end, namely, the presence of the Messiah King who comes in the name of the Lord."[26] Again the recognition and celebration of Jesus' true identity is pressed back to the beginning of the story.

In contrast to both the shepherds who spread the news of the birth and to those who hear the news with wonder and astonishment, Mary "treasured all these words and pondered them in her heart" (Luke 2:19). Not everything is given to her (see Luke 2:50); the full meaning of this experience is not instantly available to her; while all is treasured, there is much to weigh and to ponder.

The circumcision of John the Baptist happened on "the eighth day" (Luke 1:59), so now, eight days after the birth of Jesus, he is circumcised as tradition demands and, like John, is marked with the sign of the covenant (Genesis 17:11). Like John's name, so the name of Jesus is divinely given. While Matthew pauses to dwell on the significance of the name – "You will call his name Jesus, for he will save his people from their sins" (Matthew 1:21) – Luke does not alert the reader to the significance of the name, which means "The Lord saves". It is more important for Luke to mention that the angelic command to Mary to name the child Jesus, before he was conceived, is now indeed fulfilled. God's saving purpose is now taking shape.

The presentation of Jesus in the Temple

As Luke showed how Joseph and Mary were seen to fulfil the requirements of the law of Rome in travelling to Bethlehem for the census, so in this narrative they are seen to fulfil the requirements of the Mosaic Law. Five times throughout this passage Luke mentions that the observances honoured by the parents of Jesus are in accordance with the demands of the Law (2:22. 23. 24. 27. 39). Again Luke is anxious to illustrate that the beginnings of Christianity are rooted in Judaism: the parents of Jesus are no renegade figures, but devotional and observant Jews who are committed to upholding the Law, which they are seen to do in the most sacred space in Judaism. However, as signalled in Table 4.2 (page 88), if it is the Law that moves the parents of Jesus to the Temple, it is the Spirit which enables Simeon to recognise the true identity and significance of the child. Thus the Law and the Spirit come together in the Temple courts.

---

[26] Brown, *The Birth of the Messiah*, 427.

As the Gospel opened in Jerusalem so now the action returns there (2:22. 25. 38) with the first appearance of Jesus in the Temple, where he is welcomed by two representative figures from the Period of Israel, the prophet Simeon and the prophetess Anna. When the day comes for them to be purified by the Law they take Jesus up to Jerusalem. Jerusalem is the place where Jesus' saving mission will be accomplished, and when the days draw near for him to be taken up, he will resolutely take the road to Jerusalem (9:51). Luke will use the pull of Jerusalem to give shape to Jesus' ministry, just as he will give it pride of place in the resurrection narrative and the beginning of Acts. Not surprisingly, therefore, the link between Jesus and Jerusalem is an important motif in the infancy narrative.

The Law provides the occasion and the setting for moving the action from Bethlehem to the Jerusalem Temple. Luke's condensed account of the presentation and purification conflates two ceremonies: the purification of the mother and the presentation of the first-born male. In the Mosaic Law a woman was regarded as ritually unclean for forty days after the birth of a male child. At the end of that time she was required to present herself for the rite of purification by a priest; she was to make her offering to the priest at the door of the sanctuary (Leviticus 12:6ff). Although Luke speaks of "their" purification, the Law required only the mother's (Leviticus 12:2). Mary is shown to be obedient to the Law, and in its fulfilment makes the offering of the poor: two turtledoves or two pigeons.

Alongside this account Luke writes of the presentation of Jesus. The Mosaic Law held that the first-born male, both animal and human, belonged to God (Exodus 13:2). However, after the tribe of Levi dedicated themselves to the service of God, parents of the first-born were released from the requirement of the Law by an act of redemption in which they paid a ransom to the priest (Numbers 18:16). While the Law obliged the parents to pay the sum in the Temple it did not oblige them to present the child there. In Luke's account there is no mention of a ransom, perhaps because it would be inappropriate to his model of Samuel who was consecrated to the service of the Lord (1 Samuel 1:24-28).

In the story of Samuel's presentation, Elkanah and Hannah take their child to the sanctuary in Shiloh to offer him in the service of the Lord; there they are met by an aged priest, Eli, who blesses the parents of the child. Luke has already introduced us to an old couple, Elizabeth and Zechariah, whom he presented as representative figures of the *anawim;* now the aged Simeon and Anna are portrayed in similar vein, as upright and devout people who live in expectation of the consolation of Israel (see Isaiah 40:1; 66:12-13). In describing them both as prophets in a narrative with so many references to the Law, Luke might be bringing into focus the Law and the Prophets – his description of the time prior to the coming of the kingdom (16:16) – to set the scene for the manifestation of Jesus. As is clear from the sermons in Acts and the writings of Paul, however, it is the Spirit not the Law which enables people to recognise the salvation that has been brought through Jesus. So, it is that same Spirit, which Luke associates with Simeon three times, that empowers the old prophet to see salvation through Jesus.

As with the Magnificat and the Benedictus, the Nunc Dimittis is a mosaic of Old Testament texts which are recalled and set in the new context of their accomplishment in the messianic era. As Israel was ready to die when he had looked on the face of his lost son, Joseph (Genesis 46:30), so Simeon is now prepared to die because he has seen the fulfilment of the Lord's promise in Jesus. In spite of being an old man, Simeon looks forwards, not backwards, to the consolation of Israel. Now there is no reason for Simeon to wait longer, any more than there is for a watchman to stay at his post after the arrival of the one expected: the visit that was promised by God and expected by the faithful of Israel has taken place in history. Simeon's mission is completed when he can see in Jesus the Anointed of God; in a sense the old Israel can now depart in peace because a new era is beginning. Simeon's own fulfilment is bound to the fulfilment of God's plan, and that mutual fulfilment is something which Jesus expresses to his chosen: "Blessed are the eyes that see what you see! For I tell you that many prophets and kings desired to see what you see, and did not see it" (Luke 10:23-24). Simeon sees "it" in the person of Jesus.

In his canticle Zechariah blessed God because he had visited and redeemed his people; now the canticle of Simeon widens the sphere of Jesus' influence to include not only the people of Israel, but the Gentile world. Luke recounts that Mary and Joseph are astonished at what Simeon says. This might appear surprising since Mary has already been told of the stature of the child in the annunciation, and both she and Joseph have been told of the angel's annunciation to the shepherds. Why then the surprise? This has led some scholars to argue that the annunciation, the nativity and the presentation are separate traditions, none of which supposes the existence of the others. But it is possible to see the surprise of Mary and Joseph as a Lucan device to underline something of supreme importance: a prophet guided by the Spirit has just revealed to Mary and

Joseph something which has not been contained in the previous revelations: the significance of Jesus for the Gentile world.

Simeon's canticle recognises the fulfilment of Isaiah's prophecy which speaks of the day when the watchmen of the city of Jerusalem will rejoice when they see God face to face; for God is not only consoling his people but all the nations will see the salvation of God:

> Listen! Your sentinels lift up their voices,
> together they sing for joy;
> for in plain sight they see
> the return of the LORD to Zion.
>
> Break forth together into singing,
> you ruins of Jerusalem;
> for the LORD has comforted his people,
> he has redeemed Jerusalem.
>
> The LORD has bared his holy arm
> before the eyes of all the nations;
> and all the ends of the earth
> shall see the salvation of our God (Isaiah 52:8-10).

Luke does not ascribe to Jesus any missionary activity to the Gentiles and, as Jeremias argues, all the evangelists limit Jesus' activity to Israel and impose similar limitations on the disciples even though Jesus expressly promises the Gentiles a share in his kingdom.[27] For Luke, the mission to the Gentiles begins only after the resurrection when the new message will "be preached... to all nations, beginning from Jerusalem" (24:47), a message preached in the power of the Holy Spirit (Acts 1:8). In Acts, James gives an account of Simon Peter's address to the Jerusalem meeting referring to him by his Semitic name Simeon:

> Simeon has related how God first visited the Gentiles, to take out of them a people for his name (Acts 15:14).

In the old dispensation Israel was the one people chosen from all the nations (Exodus 19:5); in the new dispensation the Gentile nations are the elected source for the new people of God. And that new choice is recognised by Simeon in the Temple of Jerusalem. From Luke's order of putting Gentiles before Israel in Simeon's canticle, Edwin Freed argues to the priority of the Gentiles over Israel, one that is sustained in the writing

---

[27] See J. Jeremias, *Jesus' Promise to the Nations* (London: SCM, 1967).

of Acts.[28] Certainly, when we come to look at the frame of Luke's Gospel, we shall see how Luke pushes back the genealogy of Jesus way beyond the patriarch Abraham to Adam, the father of the whole human race, rooting Jesus in the broad perspective of the human story.

Entering a more specific note to the oracle, Simeon addresses Mary and foretells how the child will be a source of division in Israel, something which Jesus will voice in his own preaching when he refers to the division he is sent to cause in families (Luke 12:51-53). He will be the occasion for the fall of many people (see Isaiah 8:14-15) and the rise of many, and a sign destined to be rejected by Israel (Luke 2:34). As part of Israel, Mary will be part of Israel's test, and a sword will pierce her own soul (Luke 2:35).

Since being part of Jesus' family does not automatically make for discipleship, Mary will have to meet Jesus' criterion of membership of his eschatological family, which is constituted by faithfulness to the word of God: "My mother and my brothers are those who hear the word of God and do it" (8:21; see 11:28). Luke, however, does not finish this episode on the negative aspect of Jesus' mission but concludes with Anna's praise of God and her role of spreading the word about this child whose significance has just been acknowledged and whose destiny has just been foretold.

In the final verse of this narrative Luke summarises the devotion of the parents of Jesus: "When they had performed everything according to the law of the Lord, they returned into Galilee, to their own city, Nazareth" (Luke 2:39). Here the story of the infant Jesus terminates, for in the next scene he will be twelve years old.

Jesus in the Temple among the doctors

The Jerusalem/Temple motif plays an important part in the first two chapters of Luke's Gospel, as it will in the body of the Gospel and in Acts. Opening his Gospel in the Temple in Jerusalem with the old priest Zechariah, Luke has Jesus journey to Jerusalem/Temple to be acknowledged by Simeon and Anna, and journey there again, on the feast of Passover, where he asserts his primary dedication to his Father's business. The Jerusalem Temple will be the climactic scene of Jesus' temptations (Luke 4:1-13); and Luke will use Jerusalem as the focus of Jesus' journeying (9:31. 51): he heads there "because it is impossible for a prophet to be killed away from Jerusalem" (13:33). Luke states that during

---

[28] E. Freed, *The Stories of Jesus' Birth* (London: T & T Clark International, 2004), 125-127.

the last week of Jesus' life, "every day he was teaching in the Temple" (19:47); the drama of the passion is, of course, centred in the city. In the resurrection narrative Luke keeps the action focused in Jerusalem, and in his final commission to his disciples Jesus commands that they proclaim forgiveness of sins to all nations, "beginning from Jerusalem" (24:47). In the meantime the disciples are to stay in Jerusalem (24:49) until they receive the power of the Holy Spirit. Finally, after the ascension, the disciples "returned to Jerusalem with great joy; and they were continually in the Temple blessing God" (24:52-53).

The Temple in Jerusalem provides the setting for the last scene in Luke's infancy narrative: strictly speaking, this passage does not belong to the infancy narrative, since Jesus is no longer a child. Interestingly, Luke is the only evangelist to recount an incident from the hidden life of Jesus – incidents that abound in the apocryphal Gospels, such as the second-century *Infancy Story of Thomas*, which purports to recount the activity of Jesus at the ages of five (2:1), six (11:1), eight (12:2) and twelve (19:1-5), the last being a variation of this Lucan scene.[29] The Lucan passage seems strange following the literary closure of 2:40: "The child grew and became strong, filled with wisdom; and the favour of the Lord was upon him." This has led scholars like Brown and Fitzmyer to argue that this passage was added by Luke at a later stage of writing.[30] It bears some similarity to stories of the precocious childhood of famous figures, such as Moses, Cyrus of Persia, Alexander the Great and Caesar Augustus.[31] The clearest parallel is with Flavius Josephus, who speaks of his own precocity in glowing terms, and how he was consulted by the chief priests in Jerusalem:

> While still a boy about fourteen years old, I won universal applause for my love of letters, with the result that chief priests and the leading men of the city used to come to me constantly for precise information on some particulars in our ordinances.[32]

These parallels, all referring to their subjects around the age of twelve to fourteen and found in a variety of ancient writers, may have influenced Luke in crafting this story; Luke, however, clearly has his own purpose in the telling. The reader has already read the revelations about Jesus made by others – by the angel Gabriel, by the shepherds, by Simeon and by Anna – but now in this episode we hear Jesus speak for the first time about himself, revealing himself to his parents and, by extension, to all the readers. The revelation of Jesus that he must be in his Father's house, rather than at the service of his natural family, is an anticipation of Jesus' later

---

[29] See E. Hennecke & W. Schneemelcher (eds), *New Testament Apocrypha*, trans. R. McL. Wilson (London: Lutterworth, 1963), I. 392-401.

[30] See Brown, *The Birth of the Messiah*, 478-484; Fitzmyer, *The Gospel According to Luke (I-IX)*, 435-436.

[31] For a review of the stories, see R. Laurentin, *Jésus au Temple: Mystère de Pâques et foi de Marie en Luc 2:48-50* (Paris: Gabalda, 1966), 147-158.

[32] Flavius Josephus, *Life*, 2.9.

ministry when he will reflect on how he must (*dei*) fulfil the mission given him by his Father (4:43; 9:22; 13:32; 17:25).

The scene opens with the journey from Nazareth up to Jerusalem, a journey which will later form for Luke the narrative context of Jesus' public ministry, from 9:51 until 19:44. Traditionally, every male adult Jew who lived within a day's journey of Jerusalem was expected to attend the annual feasts of Passover, Pentecost and Tabernacles. All Jews tried to attend the feast of the Passover in Jerusalem at least once in their lives. Like many Palestinian Jews, Mary and Joseph went every year, and they brought Jesus with them in his twelfth year. In later customs, the Jewish boy was introduced to adulthood when he was twelve years old – he became *bar mitzvah*, a son of the Law, assuming the responsibilities and obligations to which his parents had committed him in the rite of circumcision. In going to Jerusalem, it is possible that Jesus was celebrating an earlier form of this rite of passage: he was no longer a child; he had begun the process of being a man.

The story tells us that Jesus stayed behind in Jerusalem, a decision that is surprisingly unknown either to Mary or Joseph who had started travelling back to Nazareth; to modern parents this might appear negligent on the part of Joseph and Mary. It was the custom at that time for whole villages to travel together to and from the feasts in Jerusalem: they would travel by caravan, the men and the women keeping their separate companies, until they would camp together at night. It was not until the end of the first day's travelling that Mary and Joseph realised their loss: probably, Luke's setting allows for a day's search and another day's journey back to Jerusalem.

On returning to Jerusalem, after three days, they find Jesus with the teachers in the Temple. Luke describes Jesus sitting among "the teachers" – who will be described in the public ministry as "scribes" and "lawyers". In 2:46 Jesus is not playing the precocious theologian, but is modestly "listening to them and asking them questions". In the next verse, however, the roles seem reversed because now the teachers seem to be asking the questions and they are amazed "at his understanding and his answers" (2:47). Previously, Luke has spoken of astonishment at what others have said of Jesus; now people are astonished at Jesus himself.

Given the previous revelations about Jesus – in the angel's pronouncement at the annunciation, the shepherds' story of the angels' proclamation, and the prophecy of Simeon – one might expect the parents' delight in the visible fulfilment of these prophecies; but they are astonished, an apparent incongruity that has deepened the majority of scholars' belief that this is a pre-Lucan narrative that originated outside the theological vision of Luke's infancy narrative; although Goulder argues that it is a Lucan composition.[33] The astonishment of Mary and Joseph, together with Mary's rebuke, would be understandable if this was the first inkling they had had of the true identity of their son. Mary's rebuke would be easier to read without the previous revelations about Jesus; but it also appears, however, that the sword that pierces the soul, prophesied by Simeon (2:35), is already at work. Mary's question focuses on herself and Joseph, while Jesus' reply focuses on his Father: "Did you not know that I must be in my Father's house?" (2:49). The first words attributed to Jesus are spoken in the Temple in Jerusalem and focus on his unique relationship with his Father: Jesus' first priority, his "I must", is to be where his Father wants him to be and to do as his Father commands him; his identity transcends family history.

Luke says that the parents of Jesus did not understand Jesus' saying, a reaction to Jesus' word which will happen throughout his later ministry. It is clear from Luke's Gospel that no one fully grasped the full identity of Jesus until after the resurrection. That understanding comes only when Jesus has completed his mission and when the Spirit of understanding is sent (Acts 1:8). If the wisdom and work of Jesus in this scene anticipate that of his public ministry, so the reaction of Mary and Joseph anticipates the later reaction of the disciples. Luke adds, however, the familiar note that Mary "kept all these things… in her heart", the same response which she made when the shepherds told her of what the angels proclaimed in their message (2:19).

The reunited threesome make their return journey to Nazareth, where Jesus is obedient to Joseph and Mary; so Jesus is seen to lead a normal family life until the time comes for the beginning of his public ministry. The refrain of growth rounds off the episode: Jesus will increase in wisdom and stature; but what for him is a long process of preparing for public life, is for Mary the process of preparing to let her son go and preparing to accept him as her Lord. But she keeps the words and events in her heart, which is the reaction of the true disciple. When Jesus makes his appearances after the resurrection, he will disclose the significance of the words and events which referred to himself (24:25-27. 45-46). In the meantime, everything must be pondered in the heart.

---

[33] M. Goulder, *Luke: A New Paradigm* (Sheffield: JSOT, 1989), I. 267-268.

The frame of Luke: the human story

Given the striking atmosphere of Temple piety that pervades the infancy narrative, the fact that all Luke's Jewish characters are positively drawn, and the fulfilment motif between Jesus' beginnings and the ancient hopes of Israel, one might think that Luke, like Matthew, is rooting the Jesus story firmly within the confines of Judaism. It all reads as a very Jewish story, until one comes to Luke's genealogy of Jesus, which he inserts into the framework of Mark's Gospel that he is following – between the baptism of Jesus and the temptations in the wilderness (Luke 3:23-38).

If Luke added the infancy narrative after completing the main body of the Gospel that begins with 3:1, it would mean that Luke had already included the genealogy in the Gospel proper at an earlier stage. Although Luke's genealogy has its Matthean counterpart (Matthew 1:1-17), Matthew elects to begin his Gospel with his book of genesis, celebrating Jesus at the head of the genealogy as "son of David, the son of Abraham", and then proceeding from Abraham through a list of people, to arrive at Jesus. In the complete text of Luke's Gospel as we read it, it looks as if Luke bides his time until after the baptism of the adult Jesus. Even if that were so, it has precedent in Old Testament genealogies, for example in the genealogy of Moses which is introduced some way into the narrative of Moses' adult mission (Exodus 6:14-25), just before Moses leads his people out of Egypt.

In societies that attach great importance to kinship, genealogies establish linear kinship, usually to a key figure. Genealogies by definition select a particular ancestor as the founding figure: their purpose is to establish the identity of their subject and accentuate his status, particularly where the question of lineage is important, such as in the case of kings and priests – the most frequent occurrences of genealogies in the Old Testament originate from priestly groups.[34] Both Matthew and Luke begin with naming Jesus and claiming descent for him, but while Matthew starts in descending order from the ancestral figure of Abraham and proceeds to enumerate a list of intermediate persons until the register of names arrives at Jesus, Luke goes in reverse, in ascending order, beginning with Jesus and eventually arriving at his chosen ancestral figure in Adam, the first human being, whose status is celebrated as "son of God" (3:38). Luke goes beyond the patriarchal period and the creation of the chosen people, including the names of Abraham and David among the register of ordinary ancestors.

There are notable differences between the genealogies of Matthew and Luke, not only in their range and structure, but also in the list of names:

---

[34] For a discussion on genealogy, identity and history, see R. Wilson, "The Old Testament Genealogies in Recent Research", *Journal of Biblical Literature*, 94 (1975), 168-189.

Luke has thirty-six names that are unknown not only to Matthew but unknown in the Old Testament. The differences are so marked that, as Fitzmyer states, they "resist all harmonization".[35] Neither list provides an exact record of Jesus' biological ancestry, but that is hardly their function: the purpose of the evangelists' genealogies – like all biblical genealogies – is to display the protagonist's identity and appropriate pedigree, thus accentuating his status: in that sense, genealogies are a narrative argument. Matthew's genealogy is messianic, underscoring Jesus' relation with Israel, celebrating him as the son of David and son of Abraham; Luke's genealogy stresses the human line of Jesus' ancestry as he presses the line of ancestry right back to the first human being, who is son of God. God, not Abraham, is the final name and the final word in the ancestral line that Luke provides for Jesus. In making Jesus son of Adam, it might appear that Luke is saying with Paul that we have a new Adam, the restorer of the human race, who incorporates a new humanity in himself (see Romans 5:15-18).

Situating the genealogy of Jesus after his baptism and prayer – when the voice from heaven declares, "You are my Son, the Beloved; with you I am well pleased" (Luke 3:22) – Luke now declares that this Son of God emerges from a real family tree and that he is bound by kinship ties not only to Israel but to the whole of humanity. Jesus belongs to the human story, the wide context that Luke affords him in his Gospel. Luke thus conveys to his readers that as Jesus emerges from the line of humanity, not just from the line of Abraham, so he is the saviour of the world, not just the saviour of the Jewish people; that he is in every sense "the son of Adam", the parent of all. And he comes for all people who are sons and daughters of Adam, not just sons or daughters of Abraham. It is Simeon who earlier voiced Luke's theological outlook when he recognised that Jesus had come not only as the glory of his people Israel but as "a light for revelation to the Gentiles" (2:32). As his origins are as wide as the human race, so his mission will be: thus the frame of Luke's Gospel can be drawn as wide as the human story (see Table 4.5). As Luke celebrates Jesus' Gentile origins, so he celebrates his Gentile mission: Jesus is a gift to every human being; he is for all.

---

[35] Fitzmyer, *The Gospel According to Luke (I-IX)*, 496.

Table 4.5

THE FRAME OF LUKE'S GOSPEL

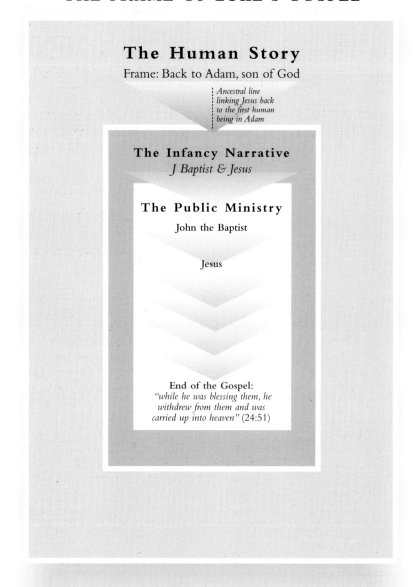

The Human Story
Frame: Back to Adam, son of God

Ancestral line linking Jesus back to the first human being in Adam

The Infancy Narrative
J Baptist & Jesus

The Public Ministry
John the Baptist

Jesus

End of the Gospel:
"while he was blessing them, he withdrew from them and was carried up into heaven" (24:51)

In keeping with his frame of the Gospel, Luke does not have Matthew's restricted mission for Jesus, "I was sent only to the lost sheep of the house of Israel" (Matthew 15:24), nor his delimitation of the disciples' mission: "Go nowhere among the Gentiles . . . but go rather to the lost sheep of the house of Israel" (Matthew 10:5-6). It is worth noting that Luke, unlike Matthew, does not include Mark's story of the Syrophoenician woman who is ignored at first by Jesus because she is not a Jew (Mark 7:24-30), an episode that is inconsistent with Luke's understanding of Jesus' gracious outreach and the wide embrace of his mission.

Hans Conzelmann's threefold division of Luke's historical perspective is well known, one where the author argues: "There is a continuity linking the three periods, and the essence of the one is carried through into the next."

1. *The Period of Israel,* running from creation to John the Baptist.

2. *The Period of Jesus,* from the beginning of his ministry to the ascension.

3. *The Period of the Church and of the Spirit,* the last age until the parousia [when the Lord will come again].[36]

While Conzelmann excludes the infancy narrative from his study of Lucan theology, Luke's infancy narrative is deliberately set within the Period of Israel, incorporating Jesus into Israel itself, and celebrating him as "the consolation of Israel" (2:25-26) and a source of "glory to your people Israel" (2:32). Throughout Luke's writing he acknowledges without regret the unique place of Israel" and its priority in salvation history, celebrating Abraham as the father of the Jews (1:73; 16:24-31). The genealogy goes further, however, incorporating Jesus into the universality of the human story, one that will be reflected in Jesus' mission statement to his followers. Luke, however, does not show any sustained mission to the Gentiles in the Period of Jesus, apart from a few episodes dealing with the Samaritans and the healing of the Gerasene demoniac. In the latter narrative, when the healed man asks Jesus if he might become a follower, Jesus declines his offer, sending him back to his own people (8:39): the time for Gentile disciples has not yet come.[37] That time will come only after the resurrection, when Luke presents the risen Jesus as the architect of the Gentile mission (see 24:47; Acts 1:8).

---

[36] H. Conzelmann, *The Theology of Saint Luke* (London: Faber & Faber, 1969), 150.

[37] For a full discussion on the question of the Gentiles in Luke's writing, see S. Wilson, *The Gentiles and the Gentile Mission in Luke-Acts* (Cambridge: CUP, 1973).

While Jesus' origins are set within the Period of Israel and his mission set within the Period of Jesus, his mission to the Gentiles will happen only through the outreach of his followers in the Period of the Church and of the Spirit. In that future, origin and mission embrace: it is in fulfilling the Gentile mission that the Church eventually catches up with the Gentile origins of its founder, embracing the whole of humanity.

Conclusion

Throughout the infancy narrative Luke absorbs a wealth of Old Testament references and subtle allusions, evidence of his conviction that the new age emerges from the old, that Christian history is intimately connected with the whole course of salvation history. As a tight summary of God's revelation the infancy narrative is the meeting place for prophecy and fulfilment, expectation and consummation; but it also has a perspective on the future in its pronouncements on the unique significance of Christ. That double perspective on the Old Testament and the Gospel is artistically maintained throughout the narrative, keeping the dramatic tension alive.

For the reader, the infancy narrative serves as a finale to the sacred history of Israel and as an overture to the Gospel: the promised visit of God has taken place in the birth of Jesus, who has been identified as the Davidic Messiah and the Son of God, the glory of Israel and a light for all peoples. When we read Luke's programmatic introduction to the public ministry of Jesus, in the visit to Nazareth, and watch how Jesus' own neighbours reject Jesus' emerging identity as prophet and teacher – instead enclosing him within the identity, "Is not this Joseph's son?" (4:22) – we realise, although we have never met the historical Jesus, that we are in the curious position of being wiser than Jesus' own neighbours. Their familiarity of knowing him as one of their own, living with him as neighbours in the small village of Nazareth, now proves to be an obstruction to understanding his true identity. Their rejection of him will prove to be a miniature of the wider rejection that is to come.

The Nazareth inhabitants may have Jesus as their teacher, but they do not have Luke as their theological guide: they have not been a privileged party to the revelations of Luke's infancy narrative, so they have no larger perspective than their immediate experience to make judgements about him. By comparison, Luke's perspective on Jesus is as wide as the human story and as deep as God's plan, hidden until now, for the salvation of all peoples.

In his infancy narrative Luke has displayed a particular interest in old people – only in his Gospel do we meet the venerable ancients in Elizabeth and Zechariah, Simeon and Anna. Although well on in years, they are not fascinated by the past, absorbed by the good old days. The poet Philip Larkin spoke of this tendency in old age when he wrote:

> Perhaps being old is having lighted rooms
> Inside your head, and people in them, acting.
> People you know, yet can't quite name: each looms
> Like a deep loss restored . . .
> > > That is where they live:
> Not here and now, but where all happened once.[38]

Luke's old people live in the here and now, primed for what is to come: what is still to happen dominates their life. They are still excited about life, about tomorrow, and what the future holds. For Luke, it is their faith, the faith of the ancients who have spent a lifetime waiting, that ushers in the new age of Gospel. Luke's old people are poets: they proclaim the Benedictus and the Nunc Dimittis. For all their wrinkles, they have never lost the capacity to wonder nor lost their desire to share their excitement in the midst of a world that has become tired of itself. They are the representatives from the Period of Israel who welcome the new things that God is doing.

Mary represents what is new and unexpected. Whatever Mary was planning for her life with Joseph, it did not include becoming pregnant outside that relationship. An unexpected word interrupts the routine of life and proposes a groundbreaking diversion from what is planned; nothing less than a startling new future is proposed. Mary gives the classic response of the disciple when challenged by the word of God: "Let it be with me according to your word" (Luke 1:38). That is her annunciation, her consent to hand over her body and spirit to God's purpose. For the story of Jesus to be told, it needs more than God's word to be spoken, it also needs the human word to say yes. That is why there are two annunciations: God's annunciation to Mary and Mary's annunciation to God. God's best plans can only happen when there is human co-operation, when God's word and the human word come together: when those two annunciations come together, God's plan begins to take shape in the womb of Mary. And when the old and the new meet together in the visitation, they honour in each other the new things God is doing.

---

[38] P. Larkin, *High Windows* (London: Faber & Faber, 1974), 19, 20.

From reading the infancy narrative there is a clear argument, furthering Luke's apologetic, that Christianity not only emerges out of Judaism but was welcomed by true representatives of Israel as the fulfilment of its own story; therefore, it has as much claim as Judaism to be recognised as a legitimate religion. Not only is it joined to Judaism, but, more importantly, its protagonist is attached to the whole of the human story: if his roots go back to Adam, so his kindly influence will reach to the ends of the earth.

5 The beginning of John

Introduction

John's Gospel is written with the declared purpose "that you may believe that Jesus is the Christ, the Son of God, and that believing this, you may have life in his name" (John 20:31). The evangelist advances his pastoral purpose by argument and affirmation, calling on a number of expert witnesses to support his lawsuit, portraying the Jews who oppose his belief in the one who comes from above – sometimes to the point of caricature – as ignorant since their father, the devil, is ruler of this world (8:44).

The Gospel is clearly marked by polemic – towards admirers of John the Baptist, towards different followers of Jesus, but, most of all, towards the group called "the Jews" who are those who reject Jesus' divine claim about himself and his mission. While the Gospel is not written to persuade these groups to become converts – it is purposefully addressed to believers not unbelievers – their hostility to John's community is such that their opposing stances must be taken into account: in facing that raw conflict, and in facing the harrowing experience of being expelled from the synagogue, the author seeks to confirm the faith of those who now believe in Jesus, to strengthen a decision that is under attack from different adversaries.

The Gospel is written in a spirit of open controversy with the synagogue. Before the destruction of the Temple in AD 70, official Judaism had tolerated the presence of Christians in the synagogue, but in the 80s there was a concerted move to expel Christians from the community: how could one be a Jew and at the same time believe that Jesus was the Christ? While Gamaliel II was president of the Jamnia assembly, around AD 85-90, formal excommunication was levelled against Jews who accepted Jesus as the Christ. As Rabbi Stephen Wylen notes:

> Rabban Gamaliel ordered another prayer added to the daily liturgy – *birkat minim,* the "blessing of the sectarians." The name is a euphemism; the prayer calls upon God to curse the sectarians. The function of this prayer was to drive the sectarians out of the synagogue, since they could hardly pray to God to bring curses down on their own heads. Modern scholars debate whether this prayer was directed specifically against Christians. We cannot know for sure. The prayer condemns all sectarians without identifying them.[1]

---

[1] S. Wylen, *The Jews in the Time of Jesus* (New York: Paulist, 1996), 187. See also. M. de Jonge, "The Conflict between Jesus and the Jews and the Radical Christology of the Fourth Gospel", *Perspectives in Religious Studies,* 20 (1993), 341-355.

Whether that insertion in the Jewish prayer or intense local opposition to the Johannine community made the effective break between the two communities is something that remains unclear. Certainly it seems doubtful that there was an unambiguous unified opposition on the part of all Jewish authorities, including those in the Diaspora, against the new Christian communities at the same time. Independent of that prayer, however, there is the clear testimony that what does dominate the thinking of the fourth Gospel is the experience of the Johannine community in being expelled from the synagogue (John 9:22; 12:42; 16:2). That expulsion catapulted the former Jewish-Christian community into the Johannine community.

The final version of the Gospel is probably written between AD 90 and 100, possibly at Ephesus. The Gospel is not known by any early second-century writer, and the earliest tradition, Irenaeus, states that the Gospel was written during the reign of Trajan (AD 98-117). The tone of the Gospel reflects the time of the writing not the time the events purportedly happened: it hardly seems comprehensible that during stage one of the tradition (the actual time of the public ministry) Jesus the Jew would have said to his own disciples, "As I said to the Jews so now I say to you…" (13:33), excluding both himself and his disciples from those who were Jews by birth. Jesus and the disciples are distinguished from "the Jews" in the sense that "the Jews" are later designated, at the time of writing, as those who reject Jesus as God's unique Son and also reject his followers. Thus by the time John writes his Gospel, the tone is one of open hostility between "the Jews" who reject Jesus and "the children of God" who accept him (see Table 5.1). Where Matthew had continuity and discontinuity between Judaism and the *ekklēsia*, where Luke had seamless continuity connecting the Period of Israel, the Period of Jesus and the Period of the Church, the evangelist John now portrays open hostility between the two designated groups.

Table 5.1

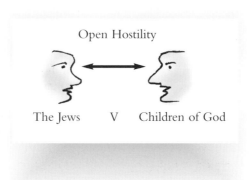

Open Hostility

The Jews   V   Children of God

By the time the fourth Gospel is written, Jews and Christians have broken off dialogue, and the Gospel language now expresses the growing hostility and sense of alienation. Following the destruction of the Temple, the rabbinic authorities had the urgent task to redefine a new Judaism that had to mature and flourish without the holy city (Jerusalem) and the holy place (the Temple); they had to develop a new sense of identity that would bind them together in a broken world, and exclude previously permitted diversity. What emerged was an orthodoxy and a sense of community that tolerated no place for those who recognised Jesus as the Messiah. That rejection gave rise to the schism between the Jews and the Christians, but as J. Painter observes: "Exclusion from the synagogue also brought self-definition to the Johannine community. . . Exclusion from the synagogue produced a community with its own identity."[2]

While Jesus and his immediate followers encountered conflict with the Jewish authorities in their own day, the separation between synagogue and those who believed in Jesus as the Messiah did not happen during the public ministry of Jesus; the evangelist projects it back into that time as a divisive issue, reinterpreting the historical roots of the problem in such a way that reflects the trauma of the community's experience. Of the seventy-one times that the term "the Jews" is used in the fourth Gospel – apart from the times when it is used as a conventional label, when, for example, the evangelist is explaining Jewish feasts – the majority of uses carry a negative meaning. One can see the relationship between "the Jews" and the Johannine community as a kind of family row between differing members about a place they have all shared and called home.[3] There is no rivalry as bitter as that between members of the same family who have separated and taken diametrically opposed stances; those who end up using invective rather than argument against one another. The fourth Gospel underlines the otherness of the Jewish tradition by referring to "the Jews" and "you Jews" and "Jewish feasts" – thus the term "Jews" is, for the most part, a hostile one.

Jewish-Christians are now estranged from their Jewish roots, from the community of believers, from a sense of belonging to the chosen people, from the Law, from the cycle of feasts, indeed from the whole rhythm of their old life. As Jewish-Christians they have been forcibly unhyphenated from their own heredity. In the atmosphere of this bitter polemic, where will they find their new identity as believers in Jesus the Christ?

The evangelist is their pastor, confirming them in the faith they have chosen, one that has excluded them from their religious past. He is also, I

---

[2] J. Painter, *The Quest for the Messiah: The History, Literature and Theology of the Johannine Community* (Edinburgh: T&T Clark, 1993), 77.

[3] See J. Ashton, "The Identity and Function of the *Ioudaioi* in the Fourth Gospel", *Novum Testamentum*, 27 (1985), 40-75.

believe, appealing to the secret Christians who, while furtively believing in Jesus, still openly remain Jews and stay attached to the synagogue. John is aware of a group of whom he writes: "Nevertheless many, even of the authorities, believed in him. But because of the Pharisees they did not confess it, for fear that they would be put out of the synagogue; for they loved human glory more than the praise of God" (John 12:42-43). While there is clearly withering criticism attached to the observation, there is also new possibility: could they be encouraged to make the break from their brethren and become open believers? Certainly three Jewish figures – the man born blind, Nicodemus and Joseph of Arimathea – are held up as religious heroes because they all overcome their past, emerge from the dark or obscurity, and attach themselves openly and publicly to the person of Jesus.

For those who have actually left behind their own religion and its traditions, John devises a spirituality of replacement: Jesus is seen to replace the Jewish Temple, the Sabbath and the feasts (Passover, Dedication and Tabernacles). A whole chapter is devoted to the man blind from birth, who is treated as a hero because his faith in Jesus leads to his excommunication from the synagogue (9:22. 34). Whereas the man's parents are so intimidated by the authorities that they refuse to acknowledge how their son received his sight, their son overcomes that intimidation, takes centre stage in the story as the protagonist, and openly berates the authorities as he acknowledges who Jesus is. All this is narrated in the context of conflict with the synagogue.

More importantly, the evangelist confronts the Jewish claim that they are the children of God. The fundamental concept of the children of God is now radically redefined: the real children of God are those who believe in Jesus the Christ. Thus the very reason why the synagogue rejects them, for believing Jesus to be the Christ, is validation for their identity as children of God. In Table 5.2 I have tried to give examples of the conflict and the divorce in the Gospel between the Jews and Jesus, between the old religion and the new community gathered around Jesus.

Table 5.2: Some example texts of the conflict

Who are the children of God? John 1:11-12	He came to his own home, and his own people received him not.	But to all who received him, who believed in his name, he gave power to become children of God.
Jesus' supremacy over Moses John 1:17-18	For the law was given through Moses;	grace and truth came through Jesus Christ. No one has ever seen God; the only Son, who is in the bosom of the Father, he has made him known.
Jewish wedding at Cana John 2:1-12	They run out of wine, but have water jars for Jewish purification.	Jesus commands jars to be filled; the water becomes the best wine.
Conflict at the Jewish Passover: Cleansing of the Temple John 2:13-25	"The Jews then said, 'It has taken forty-six years to build this temple, and will you raise it up in three days?'"	But he spoke of the temple of his body.
Conversation with Nicodemus, a Pharisee and a leading Jew John 3:1-21	Nicodemus said to him, "How can anyone be born after having grown old? Can one enter a second time into the mother's womb and be born?"	Jesus answered, "Very truly, I tell you, no one can see the kingdom of God without being born from above."
Conversation with the Samaritan woman John 4:5-30	"Our ancestors worshipped on this mountain, but you say that the place where people must worship is in Jerusalem."	"Woman, believe me, the hour is coming when you will worship the Father neither on this mountain nor in Jerusalem."
Conflict with the Jews at a Jewish festival John 5:1-21	Jesus is criticised for healing on the Sabbath. The Jews become intent on killing him.	"My Father is still working and I also am working... The Son gives life to whomsoever he wishes."
The Jewish Feast of Passover: Conflict with the Jews over bread John 6:28-59	"Our ancestors ate the manna in the wilderness."	"They died ... I am the living bread which came down from heaven, that one may eat of it and not die."
The Jewish Feast of Tabernacles John 7:37-39	During the feast, priests poured water from the pool of Siloam on the Temple altar and prayed for rain.	On the last and greatest day: "If any one thirst, let him come to me and drink." The promise of living water.
Conflict with scribes and Pharisees over the Mosaic Law John 8:1-11	"Now in the law Moses commanded us to stone such. What do you say about her?"	Jesus ignores their focus on the law, challenging them to look at their own lives. Where the law convicts the woman, Jesus liberates her.

Conflict with the Pharisees over Jesus' testimony John 8:13-20	The Pharisees said: "You are bearing witness to yourself; your testimony is not true."	"My testimony is true, for I know whence I have come and whither I am going, but you do not know."
Jesus' supremacy over Abraham John 8:31-59	The Jews said: "Abraham is our father." "Are you greater than our father Abraham, who died?"	"If God were your father, you would love me . . . You are of your father the devil... "Truly, truly, I say to you, before Abraham was, I am."
Conflict with the Pharisees over the blind man John 9	The Jews would not believe that the man had been blind and sent for his parents. His parents say, "Ask him; he is of age, he will speak for himself."	"His parents said this because they were afraid of the Jews; for the Jews had already agreed that anyone who confessed Jesus to be the Messiah, would be put out of the synagogue."
Conflict at Hanukkah, the Dedication of the Temple John 10:22-39	The altar in the Temple is re-consecrated; the Jews fetch stones to stone Jesus.	Jesus says that the Father has consecrated him and sent him into the world.
Conflict at the raising of Lazarus John 11:45-54	Chief priests and Pharisees call a meeting: "If we let him go on, everyone will believe in him." That day they resolved to kill him.	Jesus no longer went openly among the Jews, but left the district and stayed with his disciples.
Conflict with unbelieving Jews John 12:37-50	Though the Jews had been present when he gave many signs, they did not believe in Jesus.	Many did believe in him, but they did not admit it for fear of being expelled from the synagogue.
Jesus warns his disciples about future expulsion by the Jews John 16:1-4		"They will put you out of the synagogues... because they have not known the Father, nor me."
Jesus before Pilate John 18:28-40	Pilate said, "Am I a Jew? Your own nation and the chief priests have handed you over to me."	"My kingship is not of this world; if my kingship were of this world, my servants would fight, that I might not be handed over to the Jews."
Passover Preparation Day: the death of Jesus John 19:28-37	Passover lambs are killed to prepare for the feast celebrating God's deliverance of his people.	The Lamb of God who takes away the sins of the world (John 1:29) is now led out and killed. Jesus says, "It is finished."
Gathered for fear of the Jews, the disciples receive the Spirit John 20:19-23	The doors are closed in the room where the disciples are, for fear of the Jews.	The risen Jesus commissions the disciples, "As the Father has sent me, even so I send you." He breathes on them the Holy Spirit.

The final Gospel scene that mentions "the Jews" opens with the disciples behind locked doors, fearing that the Jewish authorities will persecute them as they persecuted Jesus. No doubt this scene would strike a chord with those who were torn between ties to their Jewish past and the painful isolation they would endure for believing in Jesus. The Gospel scene changes, however, and the final gift of Jesus is one that overcomes the fear of the gathered disciples: in the power of the Spirit this new community is sent, as Jesus was sent by the Father, on mission.

The portrait of Jesus – misunderstood and marginalised by the Jewish leaders, constantly in conflict with religious authority and alienated from his own people – probably articulates the experience of John's own community, now treated as strangers and outsiders from their parent group. This Gospel covers them in dignity, transforming them from being a group of expelled refugees to being a group that can take pride in its identity as the children of God. They no longer need to look to the past for a definition of who they are; they no longer need to appeal to Moses and the Law or to descent from Abraham to uncover their identity; they no longer need to explain that they are ex-Jews: their new identity is given to them by the one who came from God. Thus John, unlike the Synoptic evangelists, does not look to Judaism as a source. As Fredriksen observes:

> This radical divorce from Judaism – its people, its history, and in a more complicated way, its scripture – liberates the evangelist stylistically and theologically from composing his Gospel around biblical testimonia. The Johannine Christ is not heralded in Jewish history: he is an utterly untraditional messiah.[4]

So, who was the architect of this divorce from Judaism? Who was this evangelist? What was his community? In the decades between the public ministry of Jesus and the writing of the Gospels, clearly there are developments in the various communities that are facing different challenges and problems; there are also different ways of adapting the preached Gospel to the lived experience of the communities. No evangelist is going to ignore the situation of the community while writing the Gospel over their heads and hearts: there must, from the nature of the case, be a dialogue between the incoming tradition and the ongoing drama in the community; between what is received and what is registered. For example, in John's Gospel, unlike the Synoptics, a whole community of Samaritans, following the authoritative experience of the unnamed woman of Samaria, come to believe in Jesus and say to the woman: "It is

---

[4] P. Fredriksen, *From Jesus to Christ*, 2nd edn (New Haven: Yale University Press, 2000), 25.

no longer because of your words that we believe, for we have heard for ourselves, and we know that this is indeed the Saviour of the world" (John 4:42). Clearly, John's community has embraced a number of Samaritans,[5] who would have regarded "the Jews" as their traditional enemies, and thus made it easier for members of this new community to be expelled from the synagogue. Thus, the Samaritan presence in the community will influence the way the Gospel is written.

With regard to the fourth Gospel and its formation, three anonymous characters make their appearance: the Beloved Disciple, the evangelist and the redactor. Any theory of the formation of the Gospel is, by definition, tentative, and I would like to acknowledge the posthumously published work of R.E. Brown in this, a work edited, updated and supplemented by F.E. Moloney.[6] Brown argues for the authoritative figure of the Beloved Disciple, not an apostle, behind the writing of the Gospel. While Jews from different backgrounds could have understood Jesus differently, one of the disciples of John the Baptist, later to be idealised as the Beloved Disciple by the Johannine community, could have remembered the Jesus story in terms of light and darkness, truth and falsehood, not unlike the theological language of Qumran; he could have remembered Jesus, as reported in all four Gospels, speaking in the tradition of the Wisdom literature – and emphasised that convention, rather than, as in the Synoptic tradition, one who spoke through the medium of parables. This figure could stand behind the writing as the ancient author could give "authority" to a writing without actually committing anything to writing himself; this authoritative figure was venerated by the community; he was the one whose witness could be reliably interpreted, one of whom it is said: "He who saw it has borne witness – his testimony is true, and he knows that he tells the truth – that you also may believe" (John 19:35).

In the appendix of the Gospel, chapter 21, there is a claim written by the redactor: "This is the disciple who is bearing witness to these things, and who has written these things; and we know that his testimony is true" (John 21:24). The claim distinguishes between the "disciple" and the "we" – the "we" being an authorial group, who have responsibility for the composition of the work. The authorial "we" is hardly claiming that the disciple actually did the writing; if he did, he would have no need to include an authorial "we" in the text. More likely, it means that this disciple was the influence behind the writing, in the same way that "Pilate also wrote a title and put it on the cross . . . Pilate answered, 'What I have written I have written'" (John 19:19. 22). No one would claim that Pilate did the writing, only that he had the notice written and mounted.

---

[5] See Acts 8:14-15 where the evangelisation of Samaria is carried out by unnamed disciples; when the Twelve hear of this, they send two apostles, Peter and John, to pray with the community.

[6] R.E. Brown, *An Introduction to the Gospel of John*, ed. by F.E. Moloney (New York: Doubleday, 2003). See in particular 62-69; 78-86; 189-215.

Similarly, John 21:24 could be interpreted as the Beloved Disciple being the authority behind the writing, as supported by the phrase, "his testimony is true, and he knows that he tells the truth" (John 19:35).

At stage three of the tradition, the writing of the Gospels, Brown speaks of two key characters:

> The "evangelist" is the writer who composed the body of the existing Gospel, and "redactor" refers to another writer who made some additions after the evangelist had completed his work. Who was the evangelist and who was the redactor? ... the answer that best fits the evidence is that they were disciples of the Beloved Disciple who probably was dead by the time the Gospel was written.[7]

If, as some scholars argue, there was a Johannine school that saw the Beloved Disciple as its acknowledged leader and inspired guide, the evangelist of the fourth Gospel would have emerged from this school of preachers and given shape to the tradition about Jesus, a tradition that was to develop in open conflict with the synagogue. The original shaping of the Jesus tradition probably took place in Palestine, under the guidance of the Beloved Disciple, and continued until the 60s or 70s – possibly around the time of the Jewish War (AD 66-74) when Jews and Christians were forced to evacuate. There is evidence to suggest that the evangelist, together with a group of Johannine disciples, migrated to the Diaspora, possibly Ephesus, where the tradition was further developed, and finally brought to a close by a member or members of the school, the redactor(s). The time frame, the different geographical settings, the reinterpretation of the tradition in various situations faced by the communities, and the different writers – all this provides a number of stages over some decades and a sense of layered development in the process of the Gospel formation. The Gospel was probably published sometime in the last decade of the first century: that it was composed in Greek indicates the context in which it was written.

The tradition that Jesus was the unique Son of God, the sole revealer of the Father, inevitably forced the evangelist to rethink theology: because of who Jesus is, theology has to be reworked and God has to be understood anew. That reworking did not seem to the Jewish authorities to adhere to the principle, "The Lord our God is one" (Deuteronomy 6:4), which later led to the expulsion of the community from the synagogue.

---

[7] Brown, *An Introduction to the Gospel of John*, 78.

With the exception of chapter 21, there seems little evidence for church order or ecclesial thinking in the Gospel,[8] the emphasis being on personal relationship with Jesus: thus John stresses disciples but does not give a list of apostles, and avoids mentioning different offices. From reading 1, 2 and 3 John there emerges the clear understanding that divisions soon emerged in the Johannine community, with no distinct authority to pronounce finally on the matters arising. (For example in 3 John 9 the elder writes: "I have written something to the church; but Diotrephes, who likes to put himself first, does not acknowledge my authority.") The redactor of the fourth Gospel, aware of these new divisions, now adds an important scene in chapter 21 that supplies an authority structure in the community, one that is missing from the original Gospel text – 21:15-17 – where the unique authority of Peter is recognised and recorded. In respect to the evangelist, the redactor did not change the original ending at 20:30-31 but simply added another to bring the Gospel to a close, noting that the world itself could not contain everything that could be written about Jesus (John 21:25).

While scholars may argue that the original basic Gospel material has been edited a number of times to give us the completed text of the fourth Gospel, it has to be acknowledged that we have one final text of the Gospel – there has never been any other than the one we have to hand – and it is that final text that has been accepted into the canon as part of the New Testament. That final text – what we call the Gospel of John – is the subject of our reading and analysis.

The frames of the Gospel

Mark's outer frame went back to the eighth century BC in the prophecy of Isaiah; Matthew's outer frame went back to the nineteenth century BC in the patriarch Abraham; Luke's outer frame went back to the dawn of creation in the first human being, Adam. However various and far-reaching their outer frames, all three Gospels stay within the generous limits of creation and history, within the precincts of the human story. None of these Gospels expresses a theological belief in the pre-existence of Jesus in eternity, in his role as the creative agent of God in the formation of the world, or in God becoming incarnate in the midst of history. It is John who will go extra-terrestrial and extra-historical in asserting eternity as the true backdrop for the Jesus story.

The Jesus story in John's Gospel begins not with an adult Jesus by the river Jordan (Mark) or a newborn baby in Joseph's house in Bethlehem

---

[8] See, for example, E. Schweizer, "The Concept of the Church in the Gospels and Epistles of St John", in A. J. Higgins (ed.), *New Testament Essays in Memory of T.W. Manson* (Manchester: Manchester University Press, 1959), 230-245.

(Matthew) or a newborn lying in a borrowed manger in Bethlehem (Luke) but before the creation of the world. John's Messiah does not come from Bethlehem but from outside the realm of creation; neither can he be accurately identified as Jesus of Nazareth because he does not come from there, but from the upper realm. For John, the details of Jesus' earthly beginnings are irrelevant – no birth story is told, no mother is introduced, no time is recorded, no place is noted, no witnesses are named – because his true origin is beyond the cosmos: "In the beginning was the Word, and the Word was with God, and the Word was God." John goes back beyond the prophetic story and the Jewish story and the human story to rework Genesis and anchor the beginning of the Jesus story in the originality of God.

Independently of the Synoptic Gospels, John moves out of any historical frames and offers eternity as the real setting of his Jesus story. That is why I have not provided, as I did with the three earlier Gospels, an outer frame for the Gospel of John (see Table 5.3): there is a sense in which John breaks free of any controls and limitations to the Jesus story, passes effortlessly beyond all earthly and historical barriers, to root the Jesus story in the eternity of God – a theological perception that dominates the creeds of the Church. John provides a unique interpretative backdrop against which everything he says about Jesus must be read, summarised in the extraordinary opening verse:

> In the beginning was the Word,
> and the Word was with God,
> and the Word was God (1:1).

Everything that John writes about Jesus is subsumed under the interpretation that Jesus Christ is the eternal divine Word who was with God in the beginning: that is the interpretative key that opens up the ensuing Gospel drama. As Charles Kingsley Barrett says of this opening verse: "John intends that the whole of his Gospel be read in the light of this verse. The deeds and words of Jesus are the deeds and words of God; if this be not true the book is blasphemous."[9] Not only is Jesus' origin with God in eternity, but in the course of the Gospel narrative John's Jesus will speak out of an alert consciousness of that origin: he is in no doubt about where he comes from, who sent him, what his purpose is and whence he will return. In that sense it is true to say that the first verse of John's prologue dominates Jesus' own thinking, from his first emergence in the company of John the Baptist to the moment of his death.

---

[9] C.K. Barrett, *The Gospel According to John*, 2nd edn (London: SPCK, 1978), 156.

Table 5.3

THE FRAME OF JOHN'S GOSPEL

The Divine Story
The Logos who is God; Creator

The stranger from heaven

The Human Story

The Jewish Story

The Public Ministry
John the witness

Jesus the lamb of God

End of the Gospel:
"the world itself could not contain the books that would be written." (21:25)

The fourth evangelist does provide his Gospel, as indeed he must if he is to write a narrative, with the earthly historical frame of the world and of the human story:

> The true light, which enlightens everyone,
> was coming into the world.
> He was in the world,
> and the world came into being through him;
> yet the world did not know him (1:9-10).

As the creator of the world and the ancestor of all who live, the Word enters his own creation. The one from above descends into human history, but that entrance is not greeted with recognition or acknowledgement; he comes as a stranger from heaven.[10] John provides a double context for the Jesus story – the timeless unlimited upper realm of the divine and the limited historical setting of the lower worldly realm: this double context provides the frame for John's high Christology. The opponents of Jesus ironically observe: "Yet we know where this man comes from; and when the Christ appears, no one will know where he comes from" (John 7:27; see 9:29). That double context is something that applies not only to Jesus but to his opponents, whom Jesus addresses, "You are from below, I am from above; you are of this world, I am not of this world" (8:23).

John has another frame in the particular historical and geographical setting of his drama: the Word is destined for a particular place in the human story and for a particular people, Israel, but he is rejected by his own people:

> He came to his own home,
> and his own people received him not (1:11).

This rejection by the Jews – described as "his own people" – will be a major theme in the development of John's narrative. Given the evangelist's insistence on the eternal origins of Jesus, however, it seems not unreasonable to ask two questions. In what sense is Israel as a place Jesus' *home?* And in what sense is Jesus *Jewish?* This is not to question the undisputed historical tradition – that Jesus was a Palestinian Jew living in the first third of the first century – it is merely to question why, given John's declared Christology, he still identifies, even here in his Prologue, Jesus' home to be Israel and his own people to be Jewish. Perhaps, simply, because John has now moved into the *historical* framework of the Jesus story?

[10] See M. de Jonge, *Jesus Stranger from Heaven and Son of God* (Missoula: Scholars' Press, 1977); W. Meeks, "The Man from Heaven in Johannine Sectarianism" in *Journal of Biblical Literature*, 91 (1972), 44-72.

Yet in all four Gospels the first question Pilate asks Jesus is: "Are you the King of the Jews?"[11] In the Synoptic Gospels Jesus' reply is a variation of: "It is you who say so." In John's Gospel, however, Jesus retorts: "Do you say this of your own accord, or did others say it to you about me?", prompting Pilate's further question and observation, "I am not a Jew, am I? Your own nation and the chief priests have handed you over to me" (John 18:33-35). Jesus replies that his kingdom is *not of this world*, but like himself comes from above; if it were, his subjects would be fighting to save him "from being handed over to the Jews" (John 18:36). Jesus seems to be distancing himself from Pilate's observation that it was his "own nation" that handed him over; and Jesus' reply that his kingdom is not of this world distances himself not only from the Jews but from the whole of humanity. Jesus does not belong to this realm, an observation like so many others that makes sense only in the light of Jesus' eternal origins proclaimed in the Prologue.

The Prologue functions as an overture to the main composition of John's Gospel, introducing the main character, celebrating his relationship with God and his divine identity, and summarising the plot of what is to follow by the double theme of rejection by the Jews and welcoming belief by those who become children of God. The composition of the main narrative reflects that rejection/belief contrast: the first part is often called the *Book of Signs: Revelation to the Jews* (1:19 until chapter 12) narrating Jesus' ministry to his own people in Galilee and Judea, a ministry that is rejected; the second part, the *Book of Glory: Revelation to his Own* (chapters 13 until 20, or 21 if the appendix is included) narrating Jesus' words to those who did receive him and his return to the Father to send them the gifts that would make them God's children.

Without the Prologue, however, without the eternal backdrop that John provides for the Jesus story, it would be very difficult to make sense of the ensuing drama and the conflicts between Jesus and the Jews. The historical frame of the Gospel events is dominated by the frameless, limitless background of Jesus' origins: the information is given to us the reader, making us wiser than the participants in John's story, particularly Jesus' opponents. In that sense, John's frameless outer realm, not the historical context of the Gospel, is the key that unlocks the mystery of the Jesus story.

The Prologue

Acting as a preface to his Gospel, the Prologue offers a tight summary of John's view of Jesus as a divine being who comes into the world as an

---

[11] See Mark 15:2; Matthew 27:11; Luke 23:3.

incarnate human being, to make the Father known. Although unknown by the world he created and rejected by his own people, the rejection is not monolithic or total; those who do believe in him are empowered to become God's children. The Word that descended into the world will eventually return to the Father's side. In keeping with the tradition that the ministry of John the Baptist began before that of Jesus, the Prologue is interrupted twice to mention the identity of John and his function (1:6-8), and then to register John's testimony about Jesus after the incarnation (1:15).

From the opening of his Prologue, John establishes the context of the Jesus story as a divine story: the creative Word is the one whose true origin is with God and whose identity is divine. Unlike Matthew and Luke, the fourth evangelist has no genealogy of Jesus, since all life originates in him. The two greatest figures in Jewish tradition – the patriarch Abraham and the lawgiver Moses – are both surpassed in the person of Jesus, who is the creator and ancestor of all peoples.

The Word is from above and descends into human history. The historical setting for the remainder of the Gospel is, of course, in this world of time and place. This double context for the story of Jesus will be played out ironically throughout the whole movement of this Gospel, underscored by Jesus' rejoinder to his opponents, "You do not know where I come from."

Before announcing the Word's entry into the world, the evangelist introduces John the Baptist – although he is never called "the Baptist" in this Gospel. The wild man, who in the earlier Gospels led a popular revivalist movement that attracted all Judea and Jerusalem, is now domesticated within the fourth Gospel and is confined to playing one role: he is a witness who speaks for the light. As Meier notes of John's role in the fourth Gospel:

> His only function in the fourth Gospel is to be a witness to Jesus. Having rejected all sorts of OT titles in the opening narrative of the Gospel (1:19-22) he will accept only one OT designation: the "voice" of Isaiah 40:3, the perfect foil yet vehicle of the eternal "Word" made flesh (1:23; cf. 1:14). John's whole role in the fourth Gospel is summed up by his last directly quoted words (3:30): "He (Jesus) must increase, I must decrease." Yet none of this is a polemic against John himself, who is extolled as the first great human witness to Jesus in the Gospel; rather it is a polemic against an overly exalted estimation of John by the followers of the Baptist who later refused to become Christian.[12]

---

[12] J.P. Meier, *A Marginal Jew: Rethinking the Historical Jesus, II: Mentor, Message and Miracles* (New York: Doubleday, 1994), 119.

There is a litany of scholarly proposals for interpreting the structure of the Prologue, among them that the Prologue has a concentric chiastic structure – the first part of the structure consists of several strophes (A, B, C) that are balanced by their opposite number C', B', A'), with **D** as the pivotal statement. Among the proposals for reading the chiastic structure of the Prologue, I find the outline of J. Staley helpful:[13]

(A) The relationship of the Logos to
  1) God
  2) Creation
  3) Humankind
	vv. 1–5

(B) The witness of John (negative)	vv.6–8
(C) The journey of the Light/Logos (negative)	vv.9–11
(D) The gift of empowerment (positive)	vv.12–13
(C') The journey of the Logos (positive)	v.14
(B') The witness of John (positive)	v.15

(A') The relationship of the Logos to
  3) Humankind
  2) Re-creation
  1) God
	vv.16–18

Staley's thematic analysis groups the Prologue into lines and strophes, further grouping the strophes into larger chiastic units, thus outlining its formal structure; his further argument, relating the Prologue's symmetrical composition to the narrative structure of the body of the Gospel, need not detain us here. My own outline (Table 5.4) is much simpler, focusing not on the poetic structure of the prologue but on the dramatic theological comparison between *Logos* (the Word) and *anthrōpos* (the man), the only two Gospel characters mentioned in the Prologue, their different identities, their particular functions, a summary of their different work in the human story, concluding with the singular focus outlining the significance of the *Logos*. I think this way of seeing the Prologue accords with the primacy the evangelist accords to *Logos,* while still acknowledging the unique role of John as the first witness of the *Logos* and the spokesman for the evangelist's theology.

[13] J. Staley, "The Structure of John's Prologue: Its Implications for the Gospel Narrative Structure", *Catholic Biblical Quarterly*, 48 (1986), 249.

Table 5.4

Logos	Anthropos
Divine identity	**Human identity**
In the beginning was the Word,	There was a man sent from God,
and the Word was with God,	whose name was John.
and the Word was God.	
He was in the beginning with God.	
Function	**Function**
Creator and ancestor of all	He came for testimony,
All things came into being through him.	to bear witness to the light,
In him was life,	that all might believe through him.
and the life was the light of all people.	He was not the light,
The light shines in the darkness,	but came to bear witness to the light.
and the darkness did not overcome it.	
In human story	**In human story**
Coming into the world	John bore witness to him, and cried,
Rejection: world did not know him	"This was he of whom I said,
Rejection: own people did not accept him	'He who comes after me
Those who did become children of God.	ranks before me,
Word was made flesh, he lived among us	for he was before me.'"
and we have beheld his glory	
as the only Son from the Father.	
Significance	
And from his fullness have we all	
received, grace upon grace. For the law	
was given through Moses; grace and truth	
came through Jesus Christ. No one has	
ever seen God;	
the only Son, who is in the bosom of the	
Father, he has made him known.	

The foundational image of Jesus as *Logos,* unique to John among the writers of the New Testament, has an interesting parallel in the writing of the philosopher Philo, a contemporary of Jesus and a prominent member of the Jewish community in Alexandria, the largest Jewish settlement outside Palestine. Although widely educated in the Greek tradition, Philo was consistently loyal to Judaism and its institutions, never contradicting Jewish exegetical tradition. Philo sought to unite the insights of Greek philosophy with the biblical understanding of God's creation by using the term *Logos*. It is worth noting that he died some fifty years before the Gospel of John reached its final version. One of Philo's central ideas was *Logos,* the firstborn of God and the agent of God's creation of the world:

> To his *Logos,* his chief messenger, highest in age and honour, the Father of all has given the special prerogative to stand on the border and separate the creature from the Creator. This same *Logos* both pleads with the Immortal as suppliant for afflicted mortality and acts as ambassador of the ruler to the subject. He glories in this prerogative and proudly describes it in these words: "I stood between the Lord and you" (*Quis rerum divinarum heres* 42.205).

In borrowing from Hellenistic philosophy, Philo saw himself as a unifier between the Greek and Jewish world: *Logos* for Jew and Greek was the architect of creation, God's mental activity, his powerful word: "By the word of the Lord the heavens were made" (Psalm 33:6).[14] However, it has to be recognised that Jewish literature, being written in a Greek-influenced world, was already influenced by Hellenistic thought that had already made inroads into the Wisdom literature. As an example, Philo also uses the related concept of *Sophia,* Wisdom, which has an undisputed place in the Jewish writings; clearly this also influenced the evangelist John.[15] Probably the best example is Sirach 24, where Wisdom (*Sophia*) is personified as a woman:

> In the assembly of the Most High she will open her mouth,
> and in the presence of his host she will glory.
> "I came forth from the mouth of the Most High,
> and covered the earth like a mist.
> I dwelt in high places
> and my throne was in a pillar of cloud...
> Then the Creator of all things gave me a commandment...
> he said, "Make your dwelling in Jacob,
> and in Israel receive your inheritance."
> From eternity, in the beginning, he created me,
> and for eternity I shall not cease to exist...
> In the beloved city likewise he gave me a resting place,
> and in Jerusalem was my dominion.
> So I took root in an honoured people...
> Like a vine I caused loveliness to bud...
> Those who eat me will hunger for more...
> Those who drink me will thirst for more...
> Whoever obeys me will not be put to shame and those who work
> with my help will not sin."

---

[14] See, for example, W.A. Meeks, "The Divine Agent and his Counterfeit in Philo and the Fourth Gospel", in E. Schüssler Fiorenza (ed.), *Aspects of Religious Propaganda in Judaism and Early Christianity* (Indiana: University of Notre Dame Press, 1976), 43-67.

[15] See, in particular, Job 28; Proverbs 1 – 9; Baruch 3:9 – 4:4; Sirach (*passim*); Wisdom 6 – 10.

This personified Wisdom is a profound expression of God's creative relationship with humanity, but still she is a poetic personification, unlike the *Logos* which is uncreated, divine, and a living historical figure. Reflecting on the possible influences of Hellenistic writing and the Wisdom literature on John's use of *Logos,* Brown concludes:

> It seems that the Prologue's description of the Word is far closer to biblical and Jewish strains of thought than it is to anything purely Hellenistic. In the mind of the theologian of the Prologue the creative Word of God, the word of the Lord that came to the prophets, has become personal in Jesus who is the embodiment of divine revelation. Jesus is divine Wisdom, pre-existent, but now come among men to teach them and give them life . . . And yet, even though all these strands are woven into the Johannine concept of the Word, this concept remains a unique contribution to Christianity. It is beyond all that had gone before, even as Jesus is beyond all who have gone before.[16]

The origin of the Prologue may have been an older independent poem or hymn which was adapted by the evangelist for his own purposes. Some scholars argue that it was originally a Gnostic hymn in praise of John the Baptist, some that it was a sectarian Jewish hymn in praise of *Sophia,* others that it was a prayer of the Johannine Church, still others that it was created by the evangelist after he had finished writing the Gospel.[17] Searching for an original source might prove an interesting enterprise, but it might distract from the more immediate task of making sense of the composition as it now stands and reflecting on its place in the Gospel. We can now reflect on the individual passages that make up the Prologue.

The identity and function of the Word – *Logos* (verses 1-5)

In the beginning was the Word,
and the Word was with God,
and the Word was God.
[2]He was in the beginning with God;
[3]all things were made through him,
and without him was not anything made that was made.
[4]In him was life,
and the life was the light of men.
[5]The light shines in the darkness,
and the darkness has not overcome it.

---

[16] R.E. Brown, *The Gospel According to John* (New York: Doubleday, 1966), I. 524.

[17] For a lucid discussion on the origin and Christology of the Prologue, see J. Painter, *The Quest for the Messiah: The History, Literature and Theology of the Johannine Community* (Edinburgh: T&T Clark, 1991), 137-162.

Mark opened his Gospel with the phrase "The beginning of the Gospel", locating that beginning in the promises of God in the Old Testament; Matthew began with the Greek word *genesis*, meaning origin, tracing the genealogy of Jesus back through the Old Testament to the founding patriarch in Abraham; Luke's preface spoke of those who were eyewitnesses "from the beginning", and he went on to write his prologue in the literary style of the Old Testament, later taking the story right back to Adam, the son of God. Now John will reflect on what *he* sees is the beginning, going beyond the prophetic story of Israel, beyond the Jewish story, even beyond the human story, to before the creation of the world. Clearly all the evangelists have given thought to the idea of a beginning for the Jesus story, and none is more radical than John who believes that the Jesus story must be seen in the light of eternity.

The opening of John's Prologue is essentially a reworking of the opening of Genesis, the first book of the Torah. The Greek *en archē* echoes the opening phrase of Genesis:

> In the beginning God created the heavens and the earth. The earth was without form and void, and darkness was upon the face of the deep; and the Spirit of God was moving over the face of the deep. And God said, "Let there be light"; and there was light. And God saw that the light was good; and God separated the light from the darkness (Genesis 1:1-4).

Genesis begins with God's act of creation; John's Prologue starts even before the "beginning" of Genesis by going beyond history and creation to the eternal pre-existent *Logos*. In the light of the complete Jesus story the evangelist rewrites the story of the beginning of the world. As Jesus' farewell discourse reminds us, the glory that was given to the Son by the Father belonged to the Son "before the world was made" (John 17:5). Before the world was, the Word already existed in relationship with God; and what God was, the Word was. As Brown notes: "The Prologue says that the Word was; it does not speculate *how* the Word was, for not the origins of the Word but what the Word does is important."[18] By definition the title "Word" tells us that this divine being is destined for communication: when the Word creates, therefore, the whole of that creation acts as a revelation.

There is not a static co-existence between the *Logos* and God, but a dynamic relationship between them, a relationship that continues as the final verse of the Prologue reminds us: "the only Son, who is in the bosom of the Father". As C.H. Dodd reflects:

---

[18] Brown, *The Gospel According to John*, I. 24.

The relation of Father and Son is an eternal relation upon the field of time. It is such, not as mere reflection, or representation, of the reality, but in the sense that the love which the Father bore the Son "before the foundation of the world," and which He perpetually returns, is actively at work in the whole historical life of Jesus.[19]

The relationship of God and the Word in the Prologue, and Jesus as Son and the Father in the remainder of the Gospel, is the relationship that dominates the entire Gospel narrative; in that sense John has two protagonists in his Gospel story. Outside the Prologue, John will not use this title of *Logos*/Word again: the Word will become flesh in the person of Jesus Christ who will carry out the function of the Word in revealing the Father: "he has made him known" (1:18).

In Genesis it is God who creates; in the Prologue the Word is the creator of everything that exists: by predicating this exclusively divine function of the Word, the evangelist reiterates the identity of the Word: "the Word was God". The life that is in the Word is the light of all peoples – life and light are key words that will be developed throughout the Gospel – a life that does not remain closed within itself but is essentially life-giving; it is revelatory and relational, going beyond itself and communicating itself as illumination to all peoples.

Later Jesus will speak of himself in terms of life: "I am the way, the truth, and the life" (14:6); and he will summarise his mission in a similar vein: "I came that they may have life and have it abundantly" (10:10) – a mission that the evangelist adopts for his own writing, that "you may have life in his name" (20:31). Similarly with the theme of light, Jesus will describe himself as the Light of the world, immediately challenging all who follow him to walk not in darkness but in the light (8:12). It is the unbelieving world, those who reject Jesus, who prefer darkness to light (3:19). Those who choose to see in the light perceive not only the world but themselves differently, as Rudolf Bultmann reflects:

> Sight is not only significant in that it enables man to orientate himself in respect of objects; sight is at the same time the means whereby man understands himself in the world, the reason he does not "grope in the dark", but sees his "way". In its original sense light is not an apparatus for illumination that makes things perceptible, but is the *brightness* itself in which I find myself here and now; in it I find my way about, I find myself at home.[20]

---

[19] C.H. Dodd, *The Interpretation of the Fourth Gospel* (Cambridge: Cambridge University Press, 1968), 262.

[20] R. Bultmann, *The Gospel of John: A Commentary* (Oxford: Blackwell, 1971), 40.

Bultmann's point is well made: the light that is Christ is the true "home" of the believer, where he comes not only to enlightenment but, more fundamentally, to his true self. That arrival home is the gift of the Revealer, the giver of life and light.

Just as in Genesis God's creative word did not abolish all darkness – in creating light God separated the light from the darkness – so in the Prologue the light defines the reaches of the darkness, which cannot overpower the light. There is no attempt to describe the origin of the darkness. For all the revelatory power of the light, the darkness is not banished – probably an oblique reference to the evangelist's own world where the conflict with the synagogue has now become hardened into separation and antagonism. Nevertheless, however threatening the presence and power of this darkness, there is the robust affirmation that it has not mastered the light.

The identity and function of the man – *anthrōpos* (verses 6-8)

⁶There was a man sent from God, whose name was John. ⁷He came for testimony, to bear witness to the light, that all might believe through him. ⁸He was not the light, but came to bear witness to the light.

The evangelist moves from poetry to prose, from *Logos* to *anthrōpos*, from eternity to history, from the Word that was God to the one who is sent by God. Eternity is interrupted to introduce John. Before we read the evangelist's account of the true light's coming into the world, the evangelist presents us to the witness of that light in the brief affirmation of John's identity and function. The true light, albeit divine, is not the sole witness to itself but needs effective witnesses. As Stanley Marrow comments:

> The coming of the revelation into the world, even the coming of the Word in the flesh, does not and cannot dispense with human agency. There always has to be those who are in the world "for testimony, to bear witness to the light" (1:8). There is no other way in which "all might believe" except through others like themselves. The indispensability of human agency remains essential to divine revelation.[21]

In asserting that John is not the light, the evangelist's tone sounds suddenly defensive, ensuring his readers are aware that John is only a

---

[21] S. Marrow, *The Gospel of John: A Reading* (New York: Paulist, 1995), 9.

witness. Only Luke noted that John the Baptist's reputation was so great among the people that some wondered if he were the Christ (Luke 3:15), a wonder that may have been more widespread than the other Gospels care to admit. In John's Gospel the evangelist's denial that John was the light might be a corrective to some of John's disciples who made excessive claims for their master.

John's principal role in the fourth Gospel is modified to bearing witness to Jesus, something he does openly. As Mussner notes: "Testimony is given publicly. A witness usually appears in a law-suit and openly affirms what he has seen and heard. This public testimony by the witness has its own binding character."[22] In that sense John's Gospel can be seen as courtroom with the evangelist putting a case before the assembly "that you may believe that Jesus is the Christ, the Son of God, and that believing, you may have life in his name" (John 20:31). To argue his case the evangelist calls a number of witnesses to the stand, John being the first witness to testify. But John is not the only witness to give evidence in the evangelist's courtroom:

Jesus bears witness to what he knows and has seen (3:11)

Jesus can bear valid witness to himself (8:14)

The works that Jesus performs bear witness to him (5:36)

The Father bears witness to Jesus (5:37; 8:18)

The scriptures bear witness to Jesus (5:39)

Moses witnesses to Jesus in his writing (5:46)

The Spirit of truth will bear witness to Jesus (15:26)

The disciples are qualified to be witnesses to Jesus (15:27)

The evangelist himself bears witness to Jesus (19:35; 21:24)

The evangelist's school, in turn, bears its own witness (21:24)

John the Baptist is the first in line of a number of witnesses who will support the evangelist's case. If his purpose is testimony to Jesus, the evangelist acknowledges John the Baptist as the first true believer and the one through whom others will come to belief – possibly indicating, like the first followers of Jesus, that the first members of the Johannine community are converts from the Baptist group.

---

[22] F. Mussner, *The Historical Jesus in the Gospel of St John* (New York: Herder & Herder, 1967), 36.

As importantly, the presence of John the Baptist in these verses in the Prologue serves to anchor eternity in the human story. As F. Moloney notes: "The section (vv. 6-8) is not included simply to tell the reader about the Baptist. It does that, but more importantly, the Baptist introduces the word to history by pointing to him as the one and only light… For the reader John the Baptist is the only historical figure that has appeared so far."[23] Thus this man John, sent by God, will play a key role at the opening of the public ministry in witnessing to Jesus: "I have seen and have borne witness that this is the Son of God" (1:34). And it is appropriate that the evangelist's final mention of John in the Gospel story will be a tribute to John's effective witness: "Many came to Jesus; and they said. 'John did no sign, but everything that John said about this man was true'" (10:41).

The *Logos* in the human story (verses 9-14)

[9]The true light that enlightens every man
was coming into the world.
[10]He was in the world,
and the world was made through him,
yet the world knew him not.
[11]He came to his own home,
and his own people received him not.
[12]But to all who received him,
who believed in his name,
he gave power to become children of God;
[13]who were born, not of blood
nor of the will of the flesh
nor of the will of man,
but of God.
[14]And the Word became flesh
and dwelt among us,
full of grace and truth;
we have beheld his glory,
glory as of the only Son from the Father.

Stressing the universal mission of the Word, the evangelist notes that the light is for everyone, without exception, and solemnly announces that this true light was coming into the world. In Genesis the first words that God speaks are: "Let there be light" (Genesis 1:3) and when God sees that the light is good, he proceeds to separate the light from the darkness. In John's theology, however, the *Logos* and the light (*phôs*) are one: in that sense light

---

[23] F. Moloney, *Belief in the Word: Reading the fourth Gospel, John 1-4* (Minneapolis: Fortress, 1993), 35, 36.

is not created but exists eternally in the *Logos*, so that the *Logos* will predictably bring light into the world, because he is the light.

As light, the *Logos* will not just provide illumination, but illumine life itself. Later Jesus will speak of himself: "I am the light of the world. Whoever follows me will never walk in darkness but will have the light of life" (8:12).

The narrative advances: now in the world that had its being through him, the light cannot compel recognition but must wait on the acknowledgement of his creatures; but the creatures that had their life in the *Logos/Phôs* neither welcome the creative source of their life nor acknowledge that they themselves are creatures of this light. This will be interpreted later by Jesus, in the conversation with Nicodemus, a leading Jew, as elected unbelief, a preferential option for darkness, the stubborn refusal to believe in God's Son: "the light has come into the world and people loved darkness rather than light because their deeds were evil" (3:19).

Unrecognised by the world, the true light fares worse from his own people: if the world did not know him, his own people reject him, a theme that will dominate this Gospel. Compared to outright rejection, non-recognition might appear tolerable. Writing at a time when the Jewish-Christians of his own community have been rejected by the Jewish authorities and expelled from the synagogues, John tells his community that Jesus first endured that abrupt dismissal from his own people from the *beginning* of his life on earth; that their traumatic experience of being marginalised and forsaken by their own people was already rehearsed by the light of the world. Thus the light of the world effectively illumines the experience of those who believe in him, the children of God, by showing them that he was first spurned by his own but found acceptance in a believing community.

The notice of rejection by his own people covers the first part of the Gospel which describes the signs that Jesus performs (1:19 – 12:50); the notice of acceptance by all who did receive him covers the second part of the Gospel (13:1 – 20:31). The rejection of the light is not universal, for there are those who recognise and receive him: these are given power to become children of God. A.M. Hunter observes:

> Note that John calls believers children of God, reserving the title "Son" for Christ. These were the people who yielded him their

allegiance. In the Greek, this is literally "believed in his name". But since "name" means "revealed character" and "believe in" expresses personal trust, the phrase signifies those who confessed Jesus to be the Son of God.[24]

Their status as children of God, however, is not something they manage by themselves, nor is it granted by an institution or person: no one can confer the status of "children of God" but God alone. That status is within God's unique gift, so that in a real way the children of God are born not by human planning – "not of blood nor of the will of the flesh nor of the will of man, but of God" (1:13).

The Greek verb *eskēnōsen* means literally "pitched his tent" – which suggests a transitory stay, since the eternal Word will dwell temporarily in *sarx*, the flesh, during his earthly sojourn. Indeed the Word will become flesh, become truly human and share the finite existence of all humanity in this ultimate act of communication. When Solomon brought the ark of the covenant from the Citadel of David to the new Temple, the priests placed the ark in the Holy of Holies, and the glory of the Lord filled the Temple (1 Kings 8:1-13). Now, the evangelist proclaims, the humanity of Jesus is the new tabernacle, the place where the glory of God dwells; and at Cana in Galilee the disciples will see his glory and believe in him (John 2:11).

In pitching his tent "among us" John makes claims not only for Jesus but also for his own community: the believing Christian community, not Israel, is the final destination of the Word. As John Pryor comments: "It was not to Moses and to hardened Israel that God came to tabernacle (he pitched outside the camp), nor did he reveal his glory to them. Rather to us who are children of God through faith in Jesus Christ, among us has the incarnate Logos in all his glory come, and we have seen him."[25] The light that is ignored by the world and rejected by his own people does find an earthly home in a distinct community of believers, who will, in their turn, testify to their life-giving experience.

The Word that was with God in the beginning, the Word that was God, now takes human flesh and becomes man. This is the foundational belief on which the remainder of the Gospel rests: he is truly divine and truly human, true God and true man. The evangelist numbers himself among a corps of disciple-witnesses who beheld the glory of the only Son of the Father. This same insight opens the First Letter of John:

---

[24] A.M. Hunter, *The Gospel According to John* (London: CUP, 1975), 18.

[25] J. Pryor, *John: Evangelist of the Covenant People* (Illinois: InterVarsity Press, 1992), 10.

That which was from the beginning,
which we have heard,
which we have seen with our eyes,
which we have looked upon and touched with our hands,
concerning the word of life –
the life was made manifest,
and we saw it and testify to it . . .
that which we have seen and heard
we proclaim also to you,
so that you may have fellowship with us;
and our fellowship is with the Father
and with his Son Jesus Christ (1 John 1:1-3).

The evangelist argues a particularly modern case: that his insight comes from the authority of his personal experience. His testimony is not rooted in a dream or an idea or a credo, but in what he has seen and heard and touched: it is *that experience* which forms the basis of his proclamation. This is the same for the community in the Prologue who experienced the glory of the Son: that experience will qualify them to be witnesses to the light. Thus, for example, the Samaritan woman after her encounter with Jesus at Jacob's well can return to her community and testify from her experience about Jesus: "Many Samaritans from that city believed in him because of the woman's testimony" (4:39). The Samaritan woman is not a member of Jesus' own people, but the evangelist credits her as a witness, like John the Baptist, who leads others to believe in Jesus (10:41-42). As Edward Schillebeeckx has noted:

> Anyone who has had an experience *ipso facto* becomes himself a witness: he has a message. He describes what has happened to him. This narration opens up a new possibility of life for others, it sets something in motion. Thus the authority of experience becomes operative in the telling. The authority of experience has a narrative structure.[26]

As the Son is in relationship with the Father, so "the children of God" are those who live in relationship with the one who reveals the Father. As Pope Benedict XVI noted in the introduction to his first encyclical, *Deus Caritas Est*: "Being Christian is not the result of an ethical choice or a lofty idea, but the encounter with an event, a person, which gives life a new horizon and a decisive direction."[27] In the language of the evangelist that new event is the light come into the world; the new person is Jesus Christ.

---

[26] E. Schillebeeckx, *Christ: The Christian Experience in the Modern World* (London: SCM, 1980), 37-38.

[27] Benedict XVI, *Deus Caritas Est* [God is Love] (London: Catholic Truth Society, 2006), 3.

The *anthrōpos* in the human story (verse 15)

[15](John bore witness to him, and cried, "This was he of whom I said, 'He who comes after me ranks before me, for he was before me.'")

The one whose mission is to witness to the light testifies in the Prologue and speaks from the vantage point of the evangelist's theological outlook: there is no difference between the Christology of John the evangelist and that of John the witness; the latter testifies to the superiority of the one who follows him, a superiority based on the follower's pre-existence in eternity. As R. Kieffer remarks: "Matthew has already dared to group Jesus' preaching into five or six longer discourses in order to favour his own theological purpose; John is even bolder when he freely organises his material according to his theological views, making no stylistic difference between what Jesus, the Baptist, or he himself has to say."[28] All three voices speak from a knowledge of the truth that Jesus is from above and pre-existed all things. The one who was in eternity with God outranks the created one who was sent by God for testimony.

In the fourth Gospel John the Baptist will pose no searching questions about the identity of Jesus; he will not be portrayed as a prisoner of Herod Antipas, awaiting execution, who sends his disciples to Jesus with the question: "Are you the one who is to come, or are we to wait for another?" (Matthew 11:3). John the Baptist in the fourth Gospel will act out of the role allocated to him by the evangelist, a part in which there is no room for doubt or vacillation or ambiguity: he will perform his assigned role as the resolute witness sent by God "to bear witness to the light, that all might believe through him" (John 1:7). Thus he will play his role as witness with his own disciples, pointing Jesus out to them and identifying him as the Lamb of God (1:36). As Theissen and Merz observe:

> According to John 1:29ff., Jesus comes to John burdened with sin, but he does not bear his own sins. He is rather the Lamb of God who bears (or takes away) "the sins of the world" (1:29). There is no account of a baptism. The task of John and his baptismal activity is simply to identify Jesus as the one who baptises with the spirit.[29]

Thus John the Baptist in the Prologue will cry out to the reader what John the evangelist has already elaborated in the text: the superiority of the one who was with God in the beginning. In the fourth Gospel there is no rivalry between John and Jesus, no contest between these two spiritual colossi who command their own following among the people and have their own group of disciples. The relationship between Jesus and

---

[28] R. Kieffer, "John", in J. Barton and J. Muddiman (eds), *The Oxford Bible Commentary* (New York: OUP, 2001), 960.

[29] G. Theissen & A. Merz, *The Historical Jesus: A Comprehensive Guide* (London: SCM, 1998), 207.

John the Baptist is finally summarised by the latter in his last reported speech, when he shifts the theological imagery away from witness and speaks about his own role as the bridegroom's friend whose joy is now complete:

> He who has the bride is the bridegroom;
> the friend of the bridegroom,
> who stands and hears him,
> rejoices greatly at the bridegroom's voice;
> therefore this joy of mine is now full.
> He must increase, but I must decrease (John 3:29-30).

The unique significance of *Logos* (verses 16-18)

> [16]And from his fullness have we all received,
> grace upon grace.
> [17]For the law was given through Moses;
> grace and truth came through Jesus Christ.
> [18]No one has ever seen God;
> the only Son, who is in the bosom of the Father,
> he has made him known.

Again there is the stress on the revelatory and relational nature of the Word: from his fullness we have all received. The superabundance of grace is not something deserved by status or earned by effort; rather, it is absolute gift. Moses, as the giver of the Law, is now superseded by Jesus Christ – the first explicit mention of his name – who has brought grace and truth. While John will not use the word "grace" again in his Gospel, his presentation of the ministry and teaching of Jesus, his life and death, will be an elaboration of the grace that Jesus brings in himself.

The grace and truth that come through Jesus are contrasted to the Law that is given through Moses. The Law was given by Moses to the people, written on tablets of stone; Jesus Christ will reveal God not as words on stone but as a singular Word made flesh.

As the Word of God Jesus is both the revealer and the revealed; he brings God to earth in his person and ministry: to behold him is to behold God. As Gérard Rossé observes:

Jesus shows himself as "exegete" of the Father to the extent that he interprets his own existence and his own relationship with the Father as he lives it out in everyday life. He says that in a loud voice at the end of his public life: "Whoever sees me sees him who sent me" (John 12:45).[30]

In Jesus the revelation of God speaks its perfect communication; access to God is through the one he has sent, the incarnate Word; Jesus is the accessible doorway to the eternal God.

The negative assertion "No one has ever seen God" is absolute, without exception, when applied to created humanity – not even Moses is noted as an exception. The Book of Deuteronomy ends with an accolade to Moses, following his death and burial: "There has not arisen a prophet since in Israel like Moses, whom the Lord knew face to face" (Deuteronomy 34:10). While the evangelist recognises the unique character of Moses as the giver of the Law, the tribute of Deuteronomy, celebrating the unique face-to-face relationship between God and Moses, is effectively dismissed by John. Only God has seen God; only the Son of God, turned towards God since the beginning, can reveal who God is since the Son enjoys the unique authority that comes from being in relationship with the Father from the beginning. Marianne Thompson notes the point: "The Father-Son language of the Gospel of John is a prime example of the point that NT Christology is formulated primarily in relational terms, and that it articulates the relationship of Jesus to God and God to Jesus."[31]

The phrase "in the bosom of the Father" indicates this intimate relationship, like close fellowship at a meal. Because Jesus enjoys this unique intimacy with the Father, he is best able to make him known to all peoples. Thus the Prologue comes full circle: the hymn that opened with the assertion that the Word was "with God" and "was God" now ends with the image of intimacy, one that seems domestic and familial compared to the theological grandeur of the rest of the Prologue – that of the only Son of God in the bosom of the Father.

Conclusion

Thanks to the evangelist's Prologue, we as readers of the Gospel now know who Jesus is, where he comes from, what his mission is, how he will be received, and where he will go when he departs from this world. With this privileged information, we will appreciate the irony of so many

---

[30] G. Rossé, *The Spirituality of Communion: A New Approach to the Johannine Writings* (New York: New City Press, 1998), 13.
[31] M.M. Thompson, *The God of the Gospel of John* (Grand Rapids: Eerdmans, 2001), 51.

questions and guesses by Jesus' opponents about his origin and mission and destiny; but we should not for a moment believe, when we listen to their confused voices and foreign accents, that we are naturally quicker or brighter or shrewder in judgement than they are. We the readers have an obvious advantage over them, one that they, by historical accident, could not have shared: we have the witness and teaching of the evangelist.

It is as if the fourth evangelist has taken us the readers into his study and into his confidence to say: "Sit down for a moment because I have something important to share with you. Before you meet Jesus and John in the public ministry, permit me first to introduce them to you, so that you will know the truth about who they are, where they come from, and what their distinct roles are. I believe honestly that this will avoid endless confusion and it will not take much time. Let me, if I may, start at the beginning. In the beginning was the Word..."

Following this private instruction, we then meet the principal characters and follow the developing plot as we read the body of the Gospel.

The characters in the Gospel cannot see what we see because they are in a drama without a prologue, without John's Prologue. As readers of the Gospel we enjoy a critical advantage over the participants in the Gospel drama because we have a teacher in John who has taken us into his trust and deliberately set the stage for us, sharing his own witness by identifying the *Logos* and the *anthrōpos,* by distinguishing between the light and the witness to the light, and explaining their distinct but complementary roles. Thus we read the story in the light of our guide's understanding, which he shares with us in his Prologue.

Since the Gospel is a written document, however, we cannot question its author or invite further clarification: the transaction is not between a live storyteller and a live hearer who share the same culture and time and language, but between a Jewish writer of the first century and ourselves, whatever our diverse backgrounds, who belong to the twenty-first century. As believers in Jesus the Son of God we are still more foreign to John's world than the opponents of Jesus who inhabit his story: that should engender a little humility before the complexity of the text.

On reading the remainder of the story, we meet a host of different characters who react differently to Jesus, from suspicion and open aggression, through curiosity and fear, through belief and unbelief, through fidelity and violence, to the assured love of the Beloved Disciple. We watch the plot unfold and the conflict increase; we follow the drama through a series of quarrels and revelatory discourses; we are drawn into the contest between belief and unbelief, light and darkness, until the action inexorably reaches the cross. Then we are finally lifted up by the grandest truth that Jesus is not left for dead, but raised from the dead, appearing to his own with the message: "I am ascending to my Father and your Father, to my God and your God" (20:17). The one whose beginning was turned towards God returns to the bosom of his Father.

But after reading the Prologue, we notice a strange thing as we read the ensuing drama of this fourth Gospel. In spite of all the argument and conflict, the teaching and disclosure, the signs performed and the glory revealed, the character of Jesus does not seem to progress from what is revealed about him in the Prologue. Michael Mullins makes the point well:

> Jesus for the reader is a fully developed character from the beginning. The focus is on his relationship with the Father and carrying out the work the Father gave him to do rather than on his psychological, emotional or intellectual awareness and development. Unlike the protagonist in a drama or novel, he is not seen to develop or change and the various crises that unfold around him do not alter his perception, action, or character.[32]

It is not that the reader fails to learn anything more about Jesus beyond what is said in the Prologue: clearly the drama of the Gospel reveals more about Jesus in his dealings with, for example, his disciples, his Jewish opponents and the Roman authorities; rather it is a measure of the power of the Prologue that, from the beginning, it captures the essence of who Jesus is and the nature of his mission. The evangelist's authoritative Prologue has the first and the last word to say about the identity and mission of Jesus – the rest is commentary.

---

[32] M. Mullins, *The Gospel of John* (Dublin: Columba Press, 2003), 79.

Finale Where does the Jesus story begin?

The Gospels and the apostolic preaching about Jesus

The fact that there are four Gospels in the canon – the fourfold Gospel emerged in the second half of the second century – might lead some people to suppose that there were basic flaws in the single Gospels, which led the Church to bring together four Gospels. To spare any confusion, and to counter the criticism of heretics, why did the Church not choose one Gospel as normative for its faith? Or why did the Church not follow Tatian – the Christian apologist of the second century – and compose a Gospel harmony that would iron out all the apparent contradictions of a fourfold Gospel? Tatian's work, called the *Diatessaron*, was popular in the churches in Upper Syria until it was condemned in the fifth century, when the communities were obliged to conform to the general church practice and use the four Gospels. From the multiplicity of writings available at the time, the Church decided to include four Gospels in its canon of Christian scripture. As S. Barton comments:

> That there are four Gospels standing side by side in the canon, none of which has been subordinated to the other, is an invitation to recognise that the truth about Jesus to which the Gospels bear witness is *irreducibly plural* without being either incoherent or completely elastic.[1]

Four Gospels about the same Jesus, four different beginnings, four different frames, each Gospel being composed by a different writer from a different community facing different pastoral challenges. We have reflected on the four different prologues to the Jesus story that the evangelists offer us and the various frames into which they insert their narratives, hoping that these reflections might offer us keys to open the rest of the Gospel texts. We have not, however, reflected on the earlier preached Gospel of the apostolic Church, one that has yet another beginning, this time in the death and resurrection of Jesus. I would like to do that briefly by way of a finale.

The longest narrative in each of the written Gospels is the passion and death of Jesus. Paradoxically, the manner of Jesus' death was the most publicly attested fact of his life: Jesus did not die in his bed; he did not

---

[1] S. Barton, "Many Gospels, One Jesus?" in Markus Bockmuehl (ed.), *The Cambridge Companion to Jesus* (Cambridge: CUP, 2001), 170.

expire peacefully in his old age; he did not die from natural causes; rather, his brief public ministry was irrevocably interrupted when he was arrested, tried and executed. When Paul appears before King Agrippa and Festus, he argues to the public nature of the events surrounding Jesus' death, "for this was not done in a corner" (Acts 26:26). These things did not happen in secret behind closed doors, but in public, after due process, involving the highest religious and civil authorities in the land.

The earliest preaching had to account for the cross and the violent death Jesus endured if it were to make any redemptive sense of his mission. There seemed little point in concentrating on Jesus' teaching or mighty deeds, when the incident that dominated everyone's thinking about him was the manner of his death. Since those who first preached Jesus addressed fellow Jews, they had to concentrate on making sense of the greatest stumbling block to understanding the work of Jesus, his execution as a common criminal under Pontius Pilate, the Roman governor.

This early focus of the preached Gospel is reflected in each of the written Gospels, where the longest narrative about Jesus is his passion and death. Although there are differences in the four accounts, it is the one section in all four Gospels where there is most agreement among the evangelists. Scholars argue that the passion narratives are the oldest part of the Gospels, the oldest consecutive stories about Jesus, possibly based on liturgical recitation by the communities. As Raymond Collins notes, "History-of-tradition criticism suggests that many of the gospel traditions were shaped by liturgical narration (oral tradition in a liturgical context), if not by a liturgical reading of the text."[2] For a community that gathered to hallow the memory of Jesus, the passion story would have been retold and blended with prayers and insights from the Hebrew scriptures. The memory of the last week of Jesus' life would have been not only the most important in making sense of Jesus' mission but also foremost in the memory of the community that was left behind: a public execution has a way of overshadowing everything.

When we compare the different Gospels, preached and written (see Table 6.1), we notice from Jesus onwards that the focus of the preaching/writing changes. If the focus of Jesus' preached Gospel was the kingdom of God,[3] the apostolic preachers shift the focus of their Gospel preaching to the death and resurrection of Jesus – a shift summarised in the famous phrase of R. Bultmann, "the preacher becomes the preached". In the sermons of Peter in Acts and in the letters of Paul, their chosen beginning for the Jesus story is his death and resurrection, a beginning

---

[2] R. Collins, *Introduction to the New Testament* (London: SCM, 1983), 11.

[3] "The time is fulfilled, and the kingdom of God is at hand; repent, and believe in the Gospel" (Mark 1:15). See also Matthew 4:17; Luke 4:43; Acts 1:3.

that is changed again by the time the evangelists commit the Gospel to writing, not least because they have to do something the early preachers did not – situate the significance of Jesus inside a narrative framework of his life and mission. If preachers can proclaim summary truths, evangelists have to tell stories.

Table 6.1

Gospel	Focus
Jesus	the kingdom of God
Apostolic preachers	the death and resurrection of Jesus
Mark	the ministry; death and resurrection
Matthew and Luke	the infancy; ministry; death and resurrection
John	the prologue; ministry; death and resurrection

The importance of the death and resurrection can be seen in all the written Gospels: they are the combined target towards which the drama of each Gospel moves. That is reflected in our principal image of Jesus: the enduring image of Jesus that has dominated Christian iconography is not the newborn child in Bethlehem or the teacher of authority or the performer of mighty deeds; it is a dying man on a cross, the one who is rejected with violence. This image has its own teaching: whoever you believe Jesus to be depends on how you interpret his death.

In a sense none of us is complete until our death; the whole story cannot be told about us until we have completed it. The same is true of Jesus. More importantly, the death of Jesus is central to the understanding of who he is.

There is a development between the way Jesus presented himself in his public ministry and the way in which his followers presented him after the Easter event. In the long tradition of Israel, no one had ever been raised from death to eternal life and glory. (Elijah does not die but the Lord took Elijah up to heaven in the whirlwind – 2 Kings 2:1.) The belief that Jesus died, was buried and was then raised by God to glory is a conviction that changes everything. The resurrection was interpreted by the believing community as a dramatic victory over death, an intervention by God that vindicated the origin of the authority that Jesus claimed and revealed. A development takes place: those followers who met the risen Jesus came to realise that he was much more than they had previously understood during the public ministry.

The first Christians proclaimed the resurrection of Jesus long before they wrote about it. They proclaimed two basic truths:

Proclamation
a. that God raised Jesus from the dead
b. that the risen Jesus appeared to a number of witnesses.

The earliest example of this preached Gospel comes from Paul, around AD 57, when he writes to the Christians in Corinth – a growing community in this cosmopolitan city in the south of Greece – and summarises the Gospel which he preached to them:

> Now I should remind you, brothers and sisters, of the Good News that I proclaimed to you, which you in turn received, in which also you stand, through which also you are being saved, if you hold firmly to the message that I proclaimed to you – unless you have come to believe in vain. For I handed on to you as of first importance what I in turn had received: that Christ died for our sins in accordance with the scriptures, and that he was buried, and that he was raised on the third day in accordance with the scriptures… (1 Corinthians 15:1-4).

For Paul, there was only one Gospel: the oral proclamation of the significance of the death and resurrection of Jesus; there was only one set of scriptures, "the law and the prophets" (Romans 3:21), the writing we call either the Old Testament or the Hebrew scriptures. For Paul, the beginning of the Gospel starts with the death of Jesus – but not just with the unadorned fact of death but with an interpretation that is now part of the proclamation, that Jesus "died for our sins", and further, that this happened in accordance with the Hebrew scriptures. The Gospel summary continues in the proclamation that the buried Jesus was raised – again in accordance with the Hebrew scriptures, although Paul adduces no scriptural text to support his argument; neither, indeed, do any of the evangelists, a phenomenon that Wright observes as "the strange silence of the Bible".[4] Instead of quoting biblical texts, Paul argues from people's experience: what God did to Jesus was registered in the community by a series of appearances, the last of which, Paul claims, was the one he himself experienced.

Although Paul lists a litany of people that Jesus appeared to, he does not support his assertion with any narrative description of those appearances: the list of appearances is offered unembellished by any notice of place or

---

[4] See N. T. Wright's discussion of this biblical silence in the resurrection accounts, *The Resurrection of the Son of God* (London: SPCK, 2003), 599-615.

time or outcome, although Paul does remark, in his own case, that it was "as to one untimely born" (1 Corinthians 15:8). Paul gives us statement, not story; proclamation, not drama.

The Gospels, written some forty to seventy years after the death and resurrection of Jesus, begin their resurrection narratives with a paradox. None of them even attempts to describe the resurrection itself, what God did in raising Jesus from the dead: each of the evangelists passes over the resurrection of Jesus in discreet silence, moving from the burial of Jesus late on Good Friday – only Matthew pauses to note that the chief priests and the Pharisees place a seal on the tomb and mount a guard (Matthew 27:62-66) – to the story of the women returning to the tomb, to anoint the dead body of Jesus. While all four Gospels have detailed accounts of Jesus' ministry, his passion and his death, none of them, indeed no New Testament writing, has an account of the resurrection itself. It is as if there is a separate but shared instinct that the resurrection is beyond the range of narrative language, a collaborative acknowledgement that descriptive language could not adequately capture what God did in raising Jesus from the dead. Thus the Gospels confess the resurrection; they do not describe it. They convert the proclamation of the early Church into narrative form: the proclamation that God raised Jesus from the dead is now translated into a story of women finding the tomb empty; the proclamation that the risen Jesus appeared to a number of witnesses is now translated into stories of specific appearances. As Brown notes:

> As vivid as these proclamations were, the story form proved to be a more effective way of conveying the full impact of the resurrection. The association between the crucifixion and the resurrection needed to be fleshed out in a dramatic way so that those who were not present in Jerusalem could understand what God had done in making Jesus victorious over death. Consequently, the Gospel stories are quite different from the brief formulas preserved for us from the early preaching.[5]

How are the followers of Jesus going to communicate their new belief in him? How are they going to express their Christology? When they speak/write about Jesus, which scenes in the life of Jesus are going to become vehicles for the expression of their new understanding of who Jesus is? Scholars refer to the "christological moment",[6] meaning the event in the story of Jesus that the preacher or evangelist chooses as his particular scene to communicate to his hearer/reader the truth of Jesus' identity. Will it be:

[5] R.E. Brown, *Reading the Gospels with the Church* (Cincinnati: St Anthony Messenger Press, 1996), 66.

[6] For a discussion on this topic see J. Fitzmyer, *A Christological Catechism: New Testament Answers* (New York: Paulist, 1991), 81-93; R.E. Brown, "Christology" in R.E. Brown, J. Fitzmyer and R.E. Murphy (eds), *The New Jerome Biblical Commentary* (London: Chapman, 1992), 1354-1359.

The death and resurrection?
The baptism of Jesus?
The conception and birth of Jesus?
Some other moment?

The apostolic preachers (c. AD 33–70)   ➤death and resurrection

The resurrection becomes the principal means for interpreting the significance of Jesus' death, the new context for illuminating the cross. Through the resurrection of Jesus and the gift of the Spirit, Jesus' first followers come to believe what they could not have known before: that Jesus was the Messiah and Son of God. In the earliest preaching, the *resurrection* was the chief moment associated with the revelation of Jesus' identity. Note the following texts:

> "This Jesus God raised up, and of that we are all witnesses... God has made him both Lord and Christ, this Jesus whom you crucified" (Acts 2:32. 36).

> "And we bring you the good news that what God promised to the fathers this he has fulfilled to us their children by raising Jesus, as also it is written in the second psalm, 'Thou art my Son, today I have begotten thee.'" (Acts 13:32–33).

> "The gospel concerning his Son, who was descended from David according to the flesh and designated Son of God in power according to the Spirit of holiness by his resurrection from the dead, Jesus Christ our Lord" (Romans 1:3–4).

> "And being found in human form he humbled himself and became obedient unto death, even death on a cross. Therefore God has highly exalted him and bestowed on him the name which is above every name, that at the name of Jesus every knee should bow, in heaven and on earth and under the earth, and every tongue confess that Jesus Christ is Lord, to the glory of God the Father" (Philippians 2:7–11).

This early Christology displays a clear understanding that the revelation of the mystery of Jesus' identity was not gradually uncovered by the community but revealed *by God* in the act of raising Jesus from the dead: in raising Jesus from the dead, God revealed the true identity of his Son.

Thus the Christian community believe that Jesus is the Son of God not because they assert this but because God proclaimed it. The revelation of this mystery is associated with three characteristics:

> 1) *a divine proclamation*
>
> 2) *Jesus' identity is announced: he is Son of God*
>
> 3) *the agency of the Holy Spirit.*

These three characteristics of the revelation of Jesus' uniqueness will be associated by the first three evangelists with the moment each chooses to disclose the identity of Jesus to his readers.

The Gospel of Mark (c. AD 70) baptism

By the time the first Gospel is written, a more developed Christology is dominant: Jesus is now presented as the Messiah and Son of God during his ministry; the revelation that was first associated with the resurrection is now pushed back into the life of Jesus. As we noted earlier, wherever the evangelists begin the story of Jesus, they affirm Jesus' identity to the readers. Mark declares Jesus' identity to the reader in the first verse of his Gospel and then tells the story of this revelation at the baptism scene; but he preserves the older understanding that the fullness of Jesus' identity was not known until *after* his death. So, the first human witness to announce the mystery of Jesus is the centurion: "Truly this man was the Son of God" (Mark 15:39). In announcing to the *readers* the identity of Jesus at his baptism, Mark preserves the older tradition that this is associated with:

> 1) *a divine proclamation*
>
> 2) *Jesus' identity is announced: he is Son of God*
>
> 3) *the agency of the Holy Spirit.*

In Mark's baptism scene it is God, not any human agent, who announces the identity of Jesus, "Thou art my beloved Son; with thee I am well pleased" (Mark 1:11). Also, the agency of the Holy Spirit is mentioned, descending on Jesus like a dove.

The Gospels of Matthew and Luke (c. AD 80–85) conception

Unlike Mark, both Matthew and Luke compose infancy narratives, so they press back the announcement of Jesus' identity to the chosen beginning of their story in the conception and birth of Jesus. The ideas that early Christian preaching had applied first to the resurrection, that Mark pushed back to the baptism, are now projected further back to the angel's message to Joseph (Matthew) and to Mary (Luke). Again, the three characteristics of the revelation are present:

        1) a divine proclamation

        2) Jesus' identity is announced: he is Son of God

        3) the agency of the Holy Spirit.

The revelation of Jesus' identity is further announced to the magi (Matthew) and to the shepherds (Luke). The mystery that was originally revealed in the resurrection now begins, particularly in Matthew, to become evident to the disciples during the ministry. Matthew alters Mark and has confessions of Jesus as God's Son where Mark has none: compare Matthew 14:33 with Mark 6:51-52; and Matthew 16:16 with Mark 8:29.

The Gospel of John (c. AD 100)   ➡   pre-existence

As we saw when reflecting on the Prologue of John's Gospel, the fourth evangelist is alone among the Gospel writers in pressing back the announcement of Jesus' identity to pre-existence: "In the beginning was the Word, and the Word was with God, and the Word was God." In the light of his belief in who Jesus is, John rewrites not only the past of Jesus but the past of the world. He rewrites the beginning of Genesis in order to catch up with the new insight about the identity of Jesus and introduces the concept of the incarnation, the pre-existent divine Word being made flesh.

In John's Gospel Jesus now speaks out of the developed theology of the evangelist: he does not speak out of an understanding of himself within Judaism but from his own self-understanding as a pre-existent divine being (John 8:58; 10:30; 14:9; 17:5). As Schnackenburg notes: "What the Synoptic Jesus allows to be suspected under the veil of secrecy is openly revealed in John through his christological viewpoint."[7] Not only is Jesus fully aware of who he is, but John the Baptist and Jesus' own disciples have no problem in discerning the truth of his identity: there is no hidden Jesus in this Gospel, only one who is either accepted or rejected.

John's highly developed Christology of pre-existence and the incarnation is where the great creeds of the Church and most Christians begin to articulate their faith in Jesus, yet it is the culmination of the New Testament reflections about Jesus. The end of the Gospel tradition marks the beginning of most Christians' understanding of Jesus: John's high Christology has a way not only of dominating the creeds of the Church but of dominating most Christians' thinking about who Jesus is.

---

[7] R. Schnackenburg, *Jesus in the Gospels: A Biblical Christology* (Louisville: Westminster John Knox, 1995), 243.

Bringing the past up to date

As we can see from the development of early Christology, faith makes a journey backwards with the light of the resurrection and reinterprets not only the past of Jesus but also the past of the world. For the apostolic community who travelled around with Jesus during the ministry, the resurrection gives significance to events and stories that seemed puzzling; it opens up a whole range of meaning that was previously closed: "When therefore he was raised from the dead, his disciples remembered that he had said this; and they believed the scripture and the word which Jesus had spoken" (John 2:22). Faith penetrates the mystery of the historical Jesus and shapes all the Gospel stories. It is the risen Jesus who discloses the meaning of the historical Jesus.

The death and resurrection are not events added on to the ministry; they condition the whole telling of the story. The preached and the written Gospels do not lead up to the resurrection; they are born out of it. In that sense the Gospel begins with "alleluia" because it is a proclamation of the continuing presence of Jesus in the community: that is why every verse can be called Good News. In the Church's liturgical calendar it is Easter which makes for Christmas, not vice versa. The birth of Jesus *becomes* important because of his death and resurrection.

The process of reinterpreting the past in the light of new experience is not confined to the Gospel; it is something that we do all the time.[8] New insight and new understanding can make us recollect the past in a new way, reading it differently. We bring time to mind through our awareness of the present, our memory of the past, and our hope in the future. We can also choose to ignore the present, forget the past, and despair of the future. Although memory refers to the past and hope to the future, we remember and hope from where we are now: remembering and hoping are present activities. The present is significant as the dividing line between the past and the future, but memory and hope are present realities. Because of new experiences and new insight, the past can be reinterpreted and understood anew. So, too, the future can be looked at differently. In the Old Testament, for example, the memory of God's mighty deed in liberating his people from Egypt always gives Israel ground to hope in the future. The people eat the memory at Passover; they feed on it; it nourishes their spirit and their hope. The same becomes true for Christians in the celebration of the Eucharist, when the Christian community proclaim that Jesus influences the way they interpret time itself, the past, the present and the future: "Christ *has* died; Christ *is* risen; Christ *will* come again."

---

[8] See the section titled "Reinterpretation: bringing the past up to date", in D. McBride, *Emmaus: The Gracious Visit of God According to Luke* (Dublin: Dominican Publications, 2003), 141-145; "The Unity of Time in the Human Story", *The Month*, 240 (1979), 229-232.

Some stories become true only later, because only later does the true significance of the story emerge in the light of day. Although they look similar, there is a radical difference between knowing what takes place and understanding what is going on.

Table 6.2

What takes place	What is going on
the experience	the meaning
the fact	the interpretation
the event	the significance
"seeing and hearing"	"perceiving and understanding"
being an eyewitness to an event	testifying to its significance

More often than not, the meaning of an experience is not given at the time of the experience: the significance of an event, such as the death of Jesus, is not revealed at the time of its happening. There is no suggestion in the New Testament texts that the followers of Jesus interpreted the death of Jesus as a saving event *at the time* of the death; making sense of Jesus' violent death came later in the light of new revelation. Some experiences and events have to *wait* for meaning; the "whole story" can never be told until both experience and meaning are brought together. Thus Paul asserts fact *and* interpretation, event *and* significance, in his proclamation: "Christ died for our sins" (1 Corinthians 15:3).

Conclusion

By the time the Gospels are committed to writing, events of the past are retold in the light of the new experiences of the communities; memory is recreated to catch up with new awareness and new insight. Not only out of the new experience of resurrection faith and out of the love for who the Lord is revealed to be now, but also from the particular struggles each community is facing, the story of Jesus is reinterpreted and proclaimed in narrative. Everything that is written about Jesus is written in the light of who the evangelists believe him to be *at the time of writing* – the Christ, the Son of God; everything that is written about Jesus is written in the light of the challenges faced by the community *at the time of writing.* The story is retold from the perspective of the writer's present, not the story's past. Thus in the instruction from the Pontifical Biblical Commission, *Sancta Mater Ecclesia,* published in 1964, paragraph IX speaks of the sacred authors committing the Gospels to writing:

> ...for the benefit of the churches, with a method suited to the peculiar purpose which each (author) set for himself. From the many things handed down they selected some things, reduced others to a synthesis, (still) others they explicated as they kept in mind the situation of the churches . . . Indeed, from what they had received the sacred writers above all selected the things which were suited to the various situations of the faithful and to the purpose which they had in mind, and adapted their narration of them to the same situation and purpose.[9]

In writing their Gospel accounts the evangelists do not distance themselves from the struggles of their communities: they are believers, not forensic reporters of history; they are pastors of living communities, not archaeologists. They do not wait until the resurrection narrative before communicating their belief in Jesus, but share that belief in every sentence they write, just as they are mindful of writing the story for a particular community.

This means that wherever the evangelists begin their Gospels, wherever they choose to begin the story of Jesus – even though they elect to situate their narratives in different frames – their elected beginning is written in the light of who Jesus is revealed to be by God's proclamation. They write from the perspective of faith; they tell the story from a point of view, however distinctive their particular backgrounds and the pastoral challenges each faces, that has been inspired by God's Spirit of understanding. In one sense, that is where the Jesus story begins, in the heart that believes and understands; without that new beginning there would be no other beginnings to the Jesus story.

---

[9] Taken from the full text of the Instruction, *Sancta Mater Ecclesia,* translated and published in Fitzmyer, *A Christological Catechism: New Testament Answers,* 157-158.